COMMENTARY ON
The First Six Books
of Virgil's *Aeneid*

For our parents

Portions of the Translators' Introduction were originally published in *Epic to Novel*, by Thomas E. Maresca, and are copyright © 1974 by the Ohio State University Press.

Copyright © 1979 by the University of Nebraska Press
All rights reserved
Manufactured in the United States of America

Library of Congress Cataloging in Publication Data

Commentum super sex libros Eneidos Virgilii.
  English.
  Commentary on the first six books of Virgil's Aeneid.

  Translation of Commentum super sex libros Eneidos Virgilii.
  Also attributed to Bernard of Chartres.
  Includes bibliographical references and index.
  1. Vergilius Maro, Publius. Aeneis.
I. Bernard Silvestris, fl. 1136. II. Schreiber, Earl G. III. Maresca, Thomas E. IV. Bernardus Carnotensis, fl. 1114–1124.
PA6824.C613   873'.01   79–9138
ISBN 0–8032–4108–9

COMMENTARY ON
The First Six Books of Virgil's *Aeneid*

BY BERNARDUS SILVESTRIS

Translated, with introduction and notes,
by Earl G. Schreiber and Thomas E. Maresca

UNIVERSITY OF NEBRASKA PRESS
Lincoln and London

Contents

Preface	ix
Translators' Introduction:	
On the Allegory of the *Aeneid*	xi
Notes to the Introduction	xxxii
A Note on the Translation	xxxv
Commentary on the First Six Books	
of Virgil's *Aeneid*	1
Preface	3
Book 1	6
Book 2	16
Book 3	17
Book 4	25
Book 5	28
Book 6	31
Notes	109
Index	119

Preface

THE modern spate of scholarly interest in the career and works of Bernardus Silvestris (acknowledged in the notes to the Introduction) would be sufficient justification in itself to bring out at this time a translation of the commentary on the *Aeneid* associated with his name, but the intrinsic importance of the work itself was the original and remains the stronger incentive for so doing. For whether or not the author of the *Commentary on the First Six Books of the Aeneid* is the Bernardus who taught so successfully at Tours in the twelfth century, some other Bernardus, or only an alleged Bernardus, the commentary itself remains a crucial document of medieval literary history. It is one of the few sustained analyses of a major secular poem surviving from that period, and it differs radically from most other medieval commentaries on classical literature by going far beyond their more pedestrian series of equations for fables (for example, the sort of *Apollo id est Christus* formulas of the *Ovidius moralizatus* and similar works). It provides an opportunity to understand not only the significance of a particular poem for the High Middle Ages but also how that significance was determined, supported, and explained. In short, it gives us a chance to see a serious medieval scholar and critic at work on a text of central cultural importance.

Our work has been aided by many people and organizations, especially by W. T. H. Jackson of Columbia University, who read parts of an earlier version of the translation and made thoughtful suggestions; and by the American Academy in Rome, which, through funds provided by NEH, gave one of us a year's fellowship, during part of which this translation was completed.

TRANSLATORS' INTRODUCTION:
On the Allegory of the *Aeneid*

THREE interpretative (as opposed to scholiastic) commentaries on the *Aeneid*, those of Fulgentius (sixth century), Bernardus Silvestris (twelfth century), and Cristoforo Landino (fifteenth century) provided most of the necessary points of reference for the understanding of Virgil's poem in the Middle Ages and early Renaissance. While by no means unanimous in their understanding of details of the *Aeneid*, they agree with surprising uniformity about the general terms in which this epic must be read. First, and probably most important, in the composition of the *Aeneid* Virgil "followed Plato" and so constructed his epic that the crucial events of the narrative exemplify Platonic (or what postclassical ages thought was Platonic) doctrine. Second, the narrative of the *Aeneid*, whether read in natural or artificial order (chronologically or in the order in which Virgil disposed it—Bernardus's distinction), essentially presents a process of maturation, a growth in the hero from early heedlessness and sin to understanding and, implicitly, grace. Third, the descent to hell in the sixth book of the poem constitutes the most important point of the narrative, whether it is viewed as center or as climax: here Aeneas achieves either the understanding he needs to reach his goal or the understanding which is the goal itself. On these points Fulgentius, Bernardus, and Landino agree.

The significance of their disagreements is harder to assess. For the sake of convenience, it is useful to treat the three in chronological order, as if each treatise were a modification or adaptation for its own times of the "canonical" views of its predecessors. (While it is clear that Bernardus knew and used Fulgentius's commentary, it is much less certain that Landino was at all aware of Bernardus's work—though we believe he was.) This may be mildly untrue to the facts, but it conforms accurately to the stance of each of these critics vis-à-vis the *Aeneid:* each had to confront a work whose centrality to Western, Latin culture was undeniable and had to make sense of it in terms that his own times could comprehend and profit from. Such a historical treatment is further useful in that it highlights the centrality of Bernardus's *Commentary* in this tradition, a centrality that is as valid ideologically as it is historically.

The Middle Ages did not, of course—could not—approach the *Aeneid* without literary expectations and preconceptions, guided only by Christian insights into the heart of a pagan poem. Classical culture had already elevated Virgil to poetic immortality and had already subjected the *Aeneid* in particular to extensive annotation and exegesis, as well as to extravagant praise. Indeed, in a very real sense, Macrobius (fourth–fifth century) presents in his *Saturnalia* an attitude towards Virgil and the *Aeneid* which persists in a more generalized form as a position about poets and epic poetry well into the Renaissance. It illuminates these similarities and basic continuities merely to juxtapose a passage from the late classical Macrobius's *Saturnalia* and one from the Renaissance poet Tasso's *Discourses on the Epic Poem:*

> [Macrobius] You see—do you not?—that the use of all these varied styles is a distinctive characteristic of Vergil's language. Indeed, I think it was not without a kind of foreknowledge that he was preparing himself to serve as a model for all, that he intentionally blended his styles, acting with a prescience born of a disposition divine rather than mortal. And thus it was that with the universal mother, Nature, for his only guide he wove the pattern of his work—just as in music different sounds are combined to form a single harmony. For in fact, if you look closely into the nature of the universe, you will find a striking resemblance between the handiwork of the divine craftsman and that of our poet. Thus, just as Vergil's language is perfectly adapted to every kind of character, being now concise, now copious, now dry, now ornate, and now a combination of all these qualities, sometimes flowing smoothly or at other times raging like a torrent; so it is with the earth itself, for here it is rich with crops and meadows, there rough with forests and crags, here you have dry sand, here, again, flowing streams, and parts lie open to the boundless sea. I beg you to pardon me and not charge me with exaggeration in thus comparing Vergil with nature, for I think that I might fairly say

that he has combined in his single self the diverse styles of the ten Attic orators, and yet not say enough.[1]

[Tasso] Yet for all that, the world, which includes in its bosom so many and so diverse things, is one, one in its form and essence, one the knot with which its parts are joined and bound together in discordant concord; and while there is nothing lacking in it, yet there is nothing there that does not serve either for necessity or ornament. I judge that in the same way the great poet (who is called divine for no other reason but that, because he resembles in his works the supreme architect, he comes to participate in his divinity) is able to form a poem in which as in a little world can be read in one passage how armies are drawn up, and in various others there are battles by land and sea, attacks on cities, skirmishes, duels, jousts, descriptions of hunger and thirst, tempests, conflagrations, prodigies; there are a variety of celestial and infernal councils, and the reader encounters seditions, discords, wanderings, adventures, incantations, works of cruelty, audacity, courtesy, and generosity, and actions of love, now unhappy, now happy, now pleasing, now causing compassion. Yet in spite of all, the poem that contains so great variety of matter is one, one is its form and its soul; and all these things are put together in such a way that one has relation to the other, one corresponds to the other, the one necessarily or apparently so depends on the other that if one part is taken away or changed in position the whole is destroyed. And if this is true, the art of composing a poem is like the nature of the universe, which is composed of contraries, such as appear in the law of music, for if there were multiplicity there would be no whole, and no law, as Plotinus says.[2]

The poet is compared to nature, to God; his poem includes everything—it is a miniature of the universe. Tasso's exalted vision of the epic poet generalizes and extends Marcobius's praise of Virgil as a polymath, a philosopher, and a source of truth. In his *Commentary on the Dream of Scipio*, Macrobius explicitly links the poets Virgil and Homer with Plato and the philosophizing Cicero as "doctrinal authorities."[3] At approximately the same historical moment, Servius (who was a friend of Macrobius and appears as one of the speakers in the *Saturnalia*) in his own commentary on the *Aeneid* pictures Virgil as the same sort of omniscient being and prefaces his annotations to the sixth book with the warning that "all Virgil is full of wisdom, but especially this book, the chief part of which is taken from Homer. Some things in it are stated simply, others are taken from history, many from the exalted sciences of Egyptian philosophy and theology, so that several passages of this book have had entire treatises devoted to them."

None of these comments thus far quoted is at all specific. Servius, however much he admires Virgil's wisdom, rarely and seemingly reluctantly allegorizes or expounds that wisdom (his explanations of the golden bough and the descent to Hell are important exceptions).[4] Neither did Macrobius compile a thoroughgoing exegesis of the *Aeneid*, although in the course of the *Saturnalia* he does comment on many specific points. The lack of a systematic explanation of the poem does not seem important, however; what is important about the work of these men is the attitude they set up towards and the expectations they generated about Virgil and his *Aeneid*. The poet was a seer, a demigod, who built his poem with a wisdom analogous to the Wisdom that built the world; he was, moreover, a teacher of the order of Cicero or Plato. Reasonably then, later commentators and critics might expect to find in the *Aeneid* profound moral and philosophic truths, and they could reasonably address themselves to discovering the specific nature of those truths without fearing that they were distorting either Virgil's text or his intention.

The commentary of Fulgentius, titled briefly *De continentia Virgiliana (Concerning the Contents of Virgil)*, may strike a twentieth-century reader as crude, and even silly, but it is loyal to that sort of attitude towards Virgil, and it established patterns (or perhaps simply followed patterns already established) in Virgilian exegesis which persisted through and after the Middle Ages. Its expectations about the *Aeneid* remain, with differences in terminology, the expectations of the seventeenth century, so that a poet-critic like John Dryden, for instance, can casually remark that "the philosophy of Plato, as it is now accommodated to Christian use" is the only proper one for an epic poem, "as Virgil gives us to understand by his example."[5] In Fulgentius's view, Virgil's minor poems reveal in their allegorical content the secrets of the physical universe and the arts; the *Aeneid*, on the other hand, is essentially a moral poem which concerns itself with "the full range of human life."[6] So impressive and complex is the doctrine it contains that no expositor less intelligent than Virgil himself will do to explain it, and so Fulgentius's critical fiction obligingly provides the shade of Virgil, who tutors the ignorant Fulgentius (whom the shade condescendingly addresses as *homuncule*—"little man") about the meaning of his own poem. The situation is intrinsically comic: the fictional Fulgentius exaggeratedly abases himself before the ponderously schoolmasterly Virgil and dutifully recites the contents of the first book of the *Aeneid* to prove he has in fact read the poem and does in fact remember it before Virgil will deign to concisely explain it to him.

The interpretation of the poem, however, proceeds straightforwardly enough. The subject matter of the poem is the acquisition, nurturing, and perfection of wisdom. The shade of Virgil kindly explains to Fulgentius that this sequence corresponds in human development to birth, learning, and happiness. At this point in Fulgentius's commentary, Virgil compares these stages to the corresponding stages in the educational process. (This link between the epic and the process of formal education is a facet of the genre that also figures largely in the commentary of Bernardus Silvestris.) Fulgentius's Virgil very clearly defines the kind of wisdom in question as a philosophical rather than a theological virtue; Virgil himself was, as Fulgentius several times has him point out, a pagan and not a Christian. This explicit denial of Christian content offers an important clue not just to the understanding of epic (that seems bound up in the notion of wisdom and its affiliations with the educational process) but also to the medieval approach to secular or profane poetry generally. Fulgentius several times interjects to draw parallels between Virgil's exegesis of his own poem and some Christian doctrines; in each case, Virgil firmly denies that the specific doctrine was known to him. The parallels remain only parallels, not coincidences or foreshadowings, and what ought to be discussed in profane poetry, Virgil implies, is not Christian dogma but the highest philosophic and scientific knowledge of the pagan world.

From this point on, Fulgentius's interpretation of the *Aeneid*—or rather, the interpretation he puts in Virgil's mouth—sets a pattern from which later commentaries will scarcely deviate. The philosophical core of the *Aeneid* begins not *in medias res* but *ab ovo*, with the birth of man into the storms and dangers of the temporal world (the storm and shipwreck of book 1). The first, second, and third books describe the various vagaries and physical and mental imperfections of infancy and childhood, up to the point at which Anchises dies. The burial of Anchises represents Aeneas's release from parental control and his entrance into the life of the passions (book 4), symbolized by hunting, the storm (violent emotional disturbances), and his affair with Dido. At the urging of intelligence (Mercury), he abandons carnal love, which then falls to ashes (Dido on the funeral pyre). Having reached a more prudent age (book 5), he follows the memory of parental example and engages in exercises proper to a cultured man (the funeral games).

In the sixth book, Aeneas approaches the temple of Apollo, that is, he begins to study the mysteries of wisdom. He buries Misenus at this point because *Misenus* etymologically means vainglory, and this false pride must be abandoned before he can acquire the secrets of wisdom. The entrance to the underworld is his entrance into knowledge; here he contemplates the punishments of evildoers, the rewards of good men, and the follies of youth. Later, in seeing Dido among the shades, he reflects upon his former lust and is moved to repentance. He sees many being punished for the dreadful sin of pride. His planting the golden bough at the entrance of Elysium indicates that, when the task of learning is accomplished, it must be planted forever in the memory. *Elysium* means release, a life freed from the fear of teachers:

> Now in the Elysian fields Aeneas first sees the poet Musaeus, as it were, gift of the Muses, taller than all the others, who points out to him his father Anchises and the river Lethe—his father to remind him of the need to pursue habits of gravity, and Lethe to remind him of the need to forget the levity of boyhood. Notice the name Anchises, for Anchises in Greek is *ano scenon*, that is, living in one's own land. There is one God, the Father, King of all, dwelling alone on high, who yet is revealed whenever the gift of knowledge points the way. Notice how Anchises instructs his son: "In the beginning a spirit within strengthens heaven and earth, the watery plains, / The gleaming orb of the moon, and the Titanian stars." Here you see that, as befits God the creator, he teaches the secret mysteries of nature and shows how men's spirits are brought back again and again from life and makes clear the future.[7]

In the seventh book Aeneas arrives at Ausonia (growth in virtue) and chooses Lavinia (the way of labors) for his wife. In the eighth book he seeks the help of Evander (the good man or human goodness) and arms himself against the attacks of evil. The ninth book describes his struggle with Turnus, who represents a violent mind (*turos nus*). Juturna is the sister of Turnus and represents destruction (which lasts long: *diuturna*), both of which Aeneas must overcome. Generally speaking, the second six books show the good man, having acquired wisdom, actively struggling against vice. (For this reason, in commentaries such as Landino's, where the wisdom acquired by the hero is defined as an essentially contemplative virtue, the last six books have no real place. Landino almost totally ignores them and concentrates his attention and the emphasis of his interpretation on Aeneas's journey, culminating in the achievement of contemplative wisdom in the sixth book.)

Thus baldly stated, Fulgentius's reading of the *Aeneid* sounds far more absurd than it actually is. His ignoring of narrative causality and sequence and his consequent treatment of each book as a self-contained unit account for the greatest divergences between his interpretation and Virgil's text; but the ages-of-man theory, the view of epic as a step-by-step examination of the growth and maturation of man, which he derived from this method, persuaded and satisfied most of the Middle Ages—including such eminent minds as Petrarch's and Dante's—no doubt because he is not entirely wrong. Tracing the growth process from infancy may be a distortion, but it is a distortion of a process of intellectual maturation that is genuinely present in Virgil's text. The *Aeneid* is most definitely about—among many other things—growth in wisdom; and in linking that growth with formal education and with the ages of man, Fulgentius simply expresses a sound insight in terms congenial to his times. Moreover, while his commentary may wander fairly far from the literal meaning of Virgil's text, it is still tied to it by two main facts. The first is the assumption, shared by late classical culture and the Christian Middle Ages, that Virgil was indeed a polymath and that consequently the *Aeneid* covertly incorporated a great deal of esoteric knowledge which the man seeking true wisdom was under every obligation to search for in every way possible. The second is Fulgentius's consistently etymological mode of procedure. For him, names—proper names particularly—provide the clues to the deeper meaning of the poem, and by etymological analyses (some far-fetched in the extreme, some sound) he works out the allegory of the poem. A small example: the storm in book 1 is stirred up by Juno through the agency of Aeolus. Here is Fulgentius's Virgil's interpretation of that event:

I introduced the shipwreck as an allegory of the dangers of birth, which include both the pangs of the mother in giving birth and the hazards of the child in its need to be born. In such a need the human race the world over is involved. To let you understand this more clearly, the shipwreck is engineered by Juno, who is the goddess of birth. She then confronts Aeolus. Aeolus is Greek for *eonolus*, that is, world-destruction.[8]

Similarly, Fulgentius explains Palinurus as "wandering vision," Misenus as "vainglory," and Anchises as "the inhabitor of the father land" and uses all of these etymologies as clues to the real meaning of the episode.

It seems important to point out here that, unlike the allegory of Scripture, the allegory of the poets, as Fulgentius explains it, is a self-enclosed linguistic system. God's word is polysemous, because God in effect speaks things as well as words, so that for the interpretation of Scripture one can appeal to the nature of the thing as well as to the meaning of the word. For poets, only the meaning of the word is available, and they must build their microcosms, and critics must pursue their meanings, through the shadow of language. Narrative, the story, is the *fictum*, the made-up; the meanings of words are the real—and in poetry at least there is an intrinsic and essential continuity between the name and the thing, between the shadow and the body casting the shadow, between *verbum* and *verum*. For this reason the hinge of the comparison Macrobius drew between the *Aeneid* and the world turns on Virgil's eloquence—his style re-creates the variety of the world, and that worldly variety itself is implicitly understood to be God's rhetoric of things.

Fulgentius both insists on and struggles against the linguistic enclosures of epic. Virgil's earliest remarks in the commentary violate most of the rules of grammar and logic to isolate individual words as atoms of meaning, the essential seeds of the significance of the whole poem:

To satisfy your mind more fully on this point, there is a threefold progression in human life: first, to possess; then to control what you possess; and, third, to ornament what you control. Think of these three stages as arranged in my one verse line, as "arms," "man," and "the first." "Arms," that is, manliness, belongs to the corporeal substance; "man," that is, wisdom, belongs to the intellectual substance; and "the first," that is, a ruler (*princeps*), belongs to the power of judgment; whence this order, to possess, to control, to ornament. Thus in the guise of a story (*historia*) I have shown the complete state of man: first, his nature; second, what he learns; third, his attaining to prosperity.[9]

Bernardus Silvestris's commentary does the same thing to Virgil's sixth book: there Bernardus sets out to explain, in places, nearly every word of the text (at times, quite out of context), so that his work becomes almost an allegorical lexicon. But both commentators also push against the trap of language and attempt to break through the enclosure of epic to the reality outside it. Bernardus tries this by using analogy, and Fulgentius by his frequent appeals to the spectral Virgil to admit cognates with the truths of revelation—that is to say, with Scripture. In either case, the poem would then be susceptible to analysis according to the methods of biblical allegoresis, and the linguistic trap would be successfully sprung. The trick is not a contemptible one: Dante in his letter to Can Grande makes the claim for his poem that the spectral Virgil here implicitly rejects for his, and the results prove that the game is worth the candle. This kind of self-consciousness about its limitations—its style, its rhetoric, its form, its dependence on so inadequate a vehicle as language—seems absolutely characteristic of epic. As the supreme genre of classical and neoclassical literary theory, it is the most literary genre in the consciousness of its materials and the desire to transcend them. What epic seems always to want to do, and the writers of epic always to try, is not to manipulate words, but to shape reality; this emphasis appears consistently in the allegoresis of the *Aeneid*.

Bernardus's work is the most important and extensive commentary on the *Aeneid* produced in the later Middle Ages.[10] It continues quite clearly the attitudes and techniques of Fulgentius. Bernardus's mode of reading the *Aeneid* bears close relation to Fulgentius's (and to Prudentius's *Psychomachia*). The name of the character, place, or object furnishes the primary clue to its essence; its role in the poem is then examined in this light, and its meaning almost invariably located (as in Fulgentius) in a kind of psychomachia—Aeneas being the human soul, and everything else its affections, virtues, vices, or the temptations or maturational stages through which it must pass. The subject matter of epic still is, roughly, "the full range of human life." This is by no means to belittle the *Commentary;* on the contrary, it is a thoroughly sophisticated piece of literary criticism that shows tact and insight, respect for the literal meaning of Virgil's poem, and a consistent logic of exegesis. It may be the most important literary critical document of the Middle Ages for what it tells us about poetry and the way it was read. The commentary is really a tractate on education (compare the educational concerns of Fulgentius's commentary), filled with remarks on the parts and functions of the trivium and quadrivium, with special attention devoted to the character and office of poetry.

It is pointless to try to trace all of the lines of indebtedness between Bernardus's commentary and Fulgentius and Macrobius; it is sufficient to know that Bernardus borrowed freely from them and apparently felt few qualms about reshaping their ideas for his own purposes. His commentary extends their general attitude and approach to Virgil in elaborate detail into a consistent and unified explication of the *Aeneid*. His tone is that of an experienced teacher or lecturer expounding familiar or basic material: he is jocular and orderly; he makes transitions easily and clearly. One could speculate that his *Commentary* is compiled from lecture notes without one's being at all false to its tone or uncomplimentary to Bernardus; he was clearly an excellent teacher. A few places in the text seem to support this notion, notably Bernardus's apparent reference at one point to the shortness of time and the length of the syllabus ("We will not repeat these and entirely similar matters, or we shall not have time for matters not yet discussed")—a problem faced rather regularly by all teachers. His opening phrase, *in sua Eneide*, might also indicate that he has been previously discussing other Virgilian poems—that is, that the *Commentary* may be the sole remains of a series of lectures on all of Virgil's poetry. But this is purely speculative.

Bernardus begins his commentary by citing Macrobius to the effect that we are to observe two kinds of doctrine in the *Aeneid*, the truth of philosophy and the poetic fiction *(figmentum)*. He proceeds to investigate "the poet's intention, his mode of writing, and his objective in writing"—*"unde agat et qualiter et cur." Unde* provides the poet's intention, in this case to tell the story of the Trojan exiles, not according to the truth of history (which is found in Dares Phrygius) but in order to please Augustus. He also writes to imitate Homer, book 2 being the equivalent of the *Iliad*, books 1 and 3–12 the *Odyssey. Qualiter* explains the mode of the narration: Virgil employs artificial (*in medias res*) rather than natural (sequential) order. To explain *cur*, Bernardus remarks that poets write for the sake of utility (satirists) or delight (comic poets) or both (historic poets). We delight in seeing human experiences imitated, and we learn from these examples to seek *honesta* and to flee *illicita*. For example: from the labors of Aeneas we draw an example of endurance, from his love for Anchises and Ascanius, an example of piety; from the veneration he shows towards the gods, from the oracles he seeks, from the sacrifices he offers, from the vows and prayers he pours out, we are invited to religion. Through his immoderate love for Dido we are recalled from desire for illicit things. It is worth noting that for Bernardus these form the overt moral of the fiction and explain why the poet is narrating these events in the first place; Bernardus has not yet begun talking about the covert allegory.

These three items also serve the office of proem (to both the poem and the *Commentary*, apparently): *unde* renders the reader docile, *qualiter* benevolent, *cur* attentive. This accomplished, Bernardus turns his attention to the philosophic truth of the *Aeneid*, which is about the nature of human life. The procedure is this: under the veil of fiction (*sub integumento*), Virgil describes what the human spirit, temporarily placed in the human body, does or suffers. In this writing he employs natural order and thus observes both orders in his work, the poetic using artificial, the philosophic natural—as, seemingly, is appropriate to each. "*Integumentum vero est genus demonstrationis sub fabulosa narratione veritatis involvens intellectum, unde et involucrum dicitur*"—"The integument is a type of exposition which wraps the apprehension of truth in a fictional narrative, and thus it is also called an *involucrum*, a cover." We find the usefulness of such a work according to our knowledge of ourselves, for as Macrobius says, it is of great utility for a man to know himself. These facts explain for Bernardus the "*unde et qualiter et cur*" of the philosophic doctrine of the poem, and he now announces his intention of opening the integument of the twelve single books in sequence (in point of fact, his *Commentary* as we now have it breaks off in the middle of book 6).

Bernardus's procedure is to begin his discussion of each book by a summation of the narrative content and to follow that by a summary statement of the philosophic content, in a manner similar to Fulgentius's Virgil's summary of the content of each book before his exposition of it. Bernardus then goes into greater or lesser detail in his explanation according to no discernible pattern. Indeed, his treatment of book 6 varies even from the simple formal pattern just described: it contains little summation of any kind and takes the form of an examination of almost every important word of the text. A few generalizations are safe, however. Bernardus's exegetical technique, while refining Fulgentius's in thoroughness, subtlety, and literary sensitivity, resembles the latter's both in ignoring the causality and sequence of the plot and in being primarily etymological. The word, the name, still furnishes the essential clue to meaning. And like both Fulgentius and Macrobius, Bernardus strongly Platonizes Virgil and interprets the poem in the light of Neo-Platonic conceptions, as, for example, in his understanding Aeneas's mother, Venus, as world harmony, or in his Macrobian explanation of the descent to hell.

For Bernardus, the first book of the *Aeneid* tells of man's first age. Through Aeolus, the king of the winds who here evokes the storm at sea, we are brought to understand the birth of the child. He is called Aeolus *(eon olus = seculi interitus,* "the destruction of the real world") because at the birth of man *seculum* (that is, *vita animae,* "the life of the soul") perishes, while, depressed by the heaviness *(gravitas,* but used by Bernardus throughout with the obvious etymological connection with pregnancy, *gravidus)* of the flesh, it descends from its divinity and assents to fleshly desire. Thus Aeolus sends forth the winds because the birth of man begets commotions, that is, vices. With these he attacks the sea, that is, the human body, which is a gulf of trackless and uncrossable humors. Here already Fulgentius's techniques have been subtilized and refined. The whole phenomenon of birth has been worked out linguistically by a group of verbs possessing a common sense of producing, begetting, bringing forth, which are in turn linked to the entrance of the soul *(anima, spiritus)* into the flesh *(carnis, humor, mare)* which Bernardus expresses succinctly by the meaningful *gravitas-gravidus* pun. Moreover, Bernardus reinforces the purely linguistic link by employing a whole body of analogies, the most prominent of which in this section of the *Com-*

mentary is that of the four elements of the universe to the four humors of the body. Thus the *humor* of the sea is the *humor* of the body, and the whole seemingly farfetched allegoresis is linked finally to Virgil's text by the touchstones of wind, sea, and *humor* present in the text itself. By means of this sort of interpretation the whole poem becomes, in effect, a giant synecdoche, and Bernardus in interpreting simply enlarges from part to whole, from particular to general. Allegory does not impose itself from without but generates itself from within: because for the Middle Ages analogy is true, allegory is necessary. That is to say, allegory is simply the rhetorical mode which embodies the dialectical mode of analogy; the two are literary and philosophical avatars of each other and are properly fused in a work like the *Aeneid*, which is both literary and philosophical. Parts, as Aquinas says, correspond to parts, and analogy and allegory provide the modes of illuminating those correspondences. Analogy and allegory both offer imagistic shorthands, particulars which stand in relation to other particulars and to universals beyond them. More importantly, they validate each other: the rhetorical structure of allegory reproduces the logical structure of analogy, and that very correspondence is a further validation of both. In such a system, the meaning of the thing works to support the interpretation of the word, and Bernardus's criticism comes very close to escaping the confines of purely linguistic systematizing. It appeals outside itself—through analogy—for confirmation, even though it is finally still a closed linguistic system. The analogies themselves arise from language, and the whole interpretation depends in its totality on language: this fact explains the prominence and importance of Bernardus's synthetic puns—puns like *gravitas-gravidus, anima* as wind and soul, or *humor* as sea and element and component of personality—which linguistically join disparate areas of reference. Many of the commentary's interpretations depend upon just such linguistic ambiguities and links (which, unfortunately for the translators, are frequently clearer and far more easily expressed in Latin than in English).

Bernardus applies these logical and critical categories with some care. He knows that circumstances change cases, and his allegorizing almost never falls into the wooden equations characteristic of the psychomachia as genre. His remarks about the meaning of Aeneas indicate clearly the self-consciousness of his interpretation.

Aeneas is called the son of Anchises and Venus. Bernardus interprets Anchises as *celsa inhabitans* (loosely, the high-dweller), which he understands to be the father of all presiding over all. He understands that there are two Venuses, the lawful goddess and the goddess of wantonness, and that the lawful Venus is

> the harmony of the world, that is, the even proportion of worldly things, which some call Astrea, and others call natural justice. This subsists in the elements, in the stars, in the seasons, in living beings. [Book 1]

However, he calls the shameless Venus (the goddess of wantonness) concupiscence of the flesh because she is the mother of all fornications:

> One must remember in this book as well as in other allegorical works that there are equivocations and multiple significations, and therefore one must interpret poetic fictions in diverse ways. For example, in Martianus's book one should interpret Jove sometimes as the superior fire, sometimes as a star, and even sometimes as the Creator himself; likewise, one should interpret Saturn in some places as the star, in other places as time; similarly, one should sometimes interpret Mercury as eloquence and sometimes as the star. Hence, one must pay attention to the diverse aspects of the poetic fictions and the multiple interpretations in all allegorical matters if in fact the truth cannot be established by a single interpretation. This principle holds, therefore, in this work because the same name designates different natures, and conversely, different names designate the same nature, so that Apollo sometimes designates the sun, sometimes divine wisdom, and sometimes human wisdom; Jupiter sometimes designates fire and sometimes God; Venus sometimes designates the concupiscence of the flesh and sometimes the concord of the world (as we said above). Diverse names can signify the same thing (which is the definition of multivocation), as when both Jupiter and Anchises designate the Creator. Therefore, whenever you find Venus as the wife of Vulcan, the mother of Jocus and Cupid, interpret her as pleasure of the flesh, which is joined with natural heat and causes pleasure and copulation. But whenever you read that Venus and Anchises have a son Aeneas, interpret that Venus as the harmony of the world and Aeneas as the human spirit. Aeneas is so named as if *ennos demas*, that is, *habitator corporis*, "the inhabitant of the body". . . . *Demas* (that is, *vinculum*, "chain") indeed means the body, because the body is the prison of the spirit. Therefore Aeneas is the son of Venus and Anchises, since the human spirit comes from God through concord to live in the human body.

We have said these things about Anchises, Aeneas, and Venus because in many places in this work we will find these interpretations necessary. [Book 1]

In this manner, Bernardus continues to explain the first book of the *Aeneid* in terms of the tribulations of infancy. The second book he interprets briefly as describing boyhood and the acquisition of speech. The third book displays the weaknesses and passions of adolescence. After various misadventures, Aeneas arrives at Delos where he is warned by Apollo "to seek his ancient mother":

The two ancient mothers, that is, the two regions of Crete and Italy, are the two origins of Aeneas, the nature of the body and the nature of the spirit. We understand Crete as corporeal nature, which is the certain beginning of Aeneas's temporal life. And, ironically, Crete is so named as if *cresis theos*, that is, *iudicium divinum*, "divine judgment." For carnal nature judges badly about divine matters whenever it values divinity less than temporal things. We understand Italy (which is interpreted as *incrementum*, "growth") as divine nature, which is rationality, immortality, virtue, and knowledge. Aeneas is commanded to seek these by Apollo, that is, by wisdom, for wisdom admonishes him to love the divine. But Aeneas misunderstands the oracle, and when he is commanded to go to Italy, he seeks Crete. [Book 3]

Thus misdirected, Aeneas continues wandering and encountering various vices until his father dies.

Bernardus's treatment of book 4 provides a good example of both the subtlety and implications of his method. The whole interpretation holds together by virtue of an elaborate series of physical, emotional, and intellectual analogies which are expressed simultaneously and interchangeably by the linguistic relations of the *coct-* word forms Bernardus ubiquitously employs:

Having buried his father, Aeneas goes hunting. Driven by storms into a cave, he dallies with Dido and there commits adultery. Receiving Mercury's counsel, he abandons this disgraceful way of life. Having been abandoned, Dido burns herself to ashes and dies [*Dido vero deserta in cineres excocta et demigrat*]. . . .

By direct and allegorical narration Virgil describes the nature of young manhood. When Aeneas goes hunting after burying his father, it signifies that the person oblivious of his creator is engaged in hunting and other vain endeavors which pertain to young manhood. . . . Aeneas is driven to a cave by storms and rain, that is, he is led to impurity of the flesh and of desire by excitement of the flesh and by the abundance of humors coming from a superfluity of food and drink. This impurity of the flesh is called a cave, since it beclouds the clarity of mind and of discretion. The abundance of humors from food and drink leads to impurity of passion in the following way. In digestion [*in decoctione*] there are four humors: liquid, steam, foam, and sediment. After the humors of food and drink have been digested *[Decoctis . . . humoribus]* in the cauldron of the stomach, steam is then given off, and (as the nature of lightness demands) it ascends, and, having ascended and been collected in the arteries, it becomes less dense, moves to the brain, and produces the living powers. The liquid is condensed in the members of the body. The sediment is emitted by the lower passages through defecation, and the foam is emitted partially in sweat and partially through the sense openings. But when there is too great an abundance of foam (which happens in gluttonous eating and drinking), then it is emitted through the male member, which is nearest to and below the stomach, having first been converted into sperm, that is, the male seed. . . .

Thus the rain forces Aeneas to the cave. He is united with Dido and remains with her for a while. The public disgrace of a bad reputation does not check him, because a young man, having been snared by passion, does not know "what is beautiful, what is disgraceful, what is useful, or anything else." But after long waywardness he is warned by Mercury to leave. . . .

Mercury warns and censures Aeneas because he finds him ignoring useful endeavor, for Aeneas is "the tardy provider of the useful," and "wasteful of money." With a speech of certain censure, Mercury chides Aeneas, who leaves Dido and puts passion aside. Having been abandoned, Dido dies, and, burned to ashes, she passes away [*in cineres excocta*]. For abandoned passion ceases and, consumed by the heat of manliness, goes to ashes, that is, to solitary thoughts. [Book 4]

Superfluity of humor in nature produces rain; in man, physiologically, sperm; emotionally, lust; intellectually and morally, sin. All of these result from some form of decoction, and the ultimate fate of the libido produced is to be consumed in yet another—different and better—decoction.

Book 5, according to Bernardus, describes the nature of manhood. Having now abandoned the indulgence of youth, Aeneas now offers four exercises in virtue to God (the funeral games in Anchises' honor). The games illustrate the virtues of temperance, fortitude, prudence, and justice. At the conclusion of this book, Aeneas is warned by the image of his father that he will have to descend to hell to see him there. This means, says Bernardus, that Aeneas will have to descend to mundane things through contemplation, and thus he will see the creator (his father) because although the Creator is not in creatures, he may be known by the contemplation of creatures. At this point in the narrative, the helmsman Palinurus (whom Bernardus etymologically interprets as "wandering vision") dies. Until now, wandering vision steered the will (ship) of Aeneas, but when Aeneas guides it, Palinurus perishes.

As prologue to his explanation of the sixth book, Bernardus discusses the possible meanings of the *descensus ad inferos*, drawing heavily on Macrobius's notions in his commentary on Cicero's *Dream of Scipio*. Essentially, he understands four different kinds of *descensus*: the way of nature, the way of virtue, the way of vice, and the way of artifice. The natural way is birth, the descent of the soul into the body which, he explains at length, is properly called *infernum*. The virtuous way is that of the wise man who descends to creatures through contemplation in order to know better the creator: such were Hercules and Orpheus. The vicious way is to serve *temporalia* with the whole mind: such was Eurydice. The artificial way is, simply, magic. The integument of the sixth book describes the fourth way (Bernardus sees the death and cremation of Misenus as a magical rite, a sacrifice to demons), while the substrate of the book describes the second. Bernardus also links Aeneas's activities at this point to the process of formal education: the grove of Trivia is the study of eloquence; the three ways equal the three arts—grammar, dialectic, and rhetoric. The golden roofs of the temple are the four mathematical arts in which the gold of philosophy is contained. The faithful Achates is the habit of study. Like Servius, Bernardus links the golden bough with the study of philosophy in its two branches, theoretic and practical, and like Fulgentius he sees Aeneas's journey through hell as some sort of educational tour.

Bernardus glosses almost every word of the text in places in a detailed expansion and explanation of Aeneas's descent as the contemplative descent of the wise man to an examination of creatures. Essentially—and this is perhaps the most important aspect of his *Commentary*—he sees Aeneas's descent with the Sibyl and his progress through the lower world up to his entrance into the Elysian fields as a recapitulation of what has preceded in the poem. Just as the spirit descended into matter at birth (a descent to hell in itself: the natural way), the mind now descends to a contemplation of creatures and reviews the paths it has taken and the errors it has committed: thus the meetings with Trojan heroes, thus the encounter with Dido. The Sibyl herself functions as and is to be understood in a way similar to Boethius's Lady Philosophy, guiding Aeneas to an understanding of his past mistakes.[11] The purpose of this journey is to free Aeneas from his bondage to creatures by a thorough knowledge of them, so that he may pass on to see the creator (that is, Anchises). This is the circular motion of thought as conceived by medieval speculation: the mind descends from God into creatures and proceeds through a contemplation of creatures to return to God again.[12] This circular pattern forms the core of Bernardus's understanding of the *Aeneid:* it is for him a poem about the acquisition of wisdom which re-creates in itself the form of the process it describes. This notion provides the basis for his explanation of the first half of the poem, and he recapitulates it in his interpretation of the first half of book 6 and again, more briefly, in his allegorizations of the myths of Orpheus and Eurydice and of Castor and Pollux, both of which he understands as expressing the relations of soul and body, divine mind and infernal matter.

Bernardus's *Commentary* breaks off before Aeneas enters the fields of the blest and sees Anchises, but from its similarities to Fulgentius and from the exegetical patterns he has already set up, we can readily see the probable outlines of the remainder of his allegory: having acquired knowledge of terrestrial matters, Aeneas will obtain from Anchises the requisite celestial lore to return to his earthly life and, in yet another recapitulation, triumph over those vices and material forces to which he had earlier fallen victim so that, after the conclusion of Virgil's poem, he will be ready to ascend once again to God as the reward of his achieved virtues. (So at least Maphius Vegius understood the poem in the fifteenth century when he wrote a thirteenth book, explicitly giving Aeneas the apotheosis he seems to have earned.) Aeneas will choose as his wife Lavinia, the way of labors, rather than Dido, the way of pleasure.

The pattern seems quite simple, quite clear. Aeneas accomplishes his first *descensus ad inferos* by birth, as all men must, and he continues it throughout his minority by succumbing to a series of vices: these are Bernardus's first and third ways. In the sixth book, he once again descends to hell, this time according to Bernardus's second and fourth ways, by contemplation and by magic. This time, of course, a conversion takes place, and Aeneas comes to a recognition of his failings and begins to mend them. Consequently, in the same book he begins an ascent to God—contemplatively here—which will be later continued and confirmed when he returns to active life and triumphs over the vices and trials that previously defeated him. The Sibyl makes this aspect of things explicit when she warns Aeneas that he shall again have to fight Greeks, again encounter an Achilles, see another Simois and Xanthus and Doric camp—again because of a foreign bride, another Helen (*Aeneid* 6. 83–94). So the second half of the *Aeneid* is in effect a repetition of the first half, with the important difference that the direction of the narrative and of Aeneas's fortunes is upwards rather than downwards, ascent towards God rather than descent to creatures. This sixth book functions as the nexus, the conversion point, which terminates one journey and transforms it into its mirror image—all of which is not in any structural particular untrue to Virgil's text. However much of our understanding of the events of the *Aeneid* may differ from Bernardus's, we can hardly quarrel with his perception of its structure.

Cristoforo Landino's immensely important *Disputationes Camaldulenses* both continues and modifies this kind of reading of the *Aeneid*.[13] Landino's commentary on the *Aeneid*, which he puts in the mouth of Leone Battista Alberti, forms books 3 and 4 of the *Disputations* and is designed to be a lengthy demonstration of the superiority of the contemplative life to the active—this having been the thesis and conclusion of the first two books. Landino makes utterly explicit what is already clear in Fulgentius and Bernardus: Virgil in the *Aeneid* is exemplifying and illustrating Platonic doctrine. Like Fulgentius and Bernardus, Landino begins his allegorization *ab ovo*, with "the first age of man." Unlike them Landino does not start with book 1 of the poem, but rather with the chronologically earliest events in the poem, Aeneas's recollections of Troy. From that point he proceeds through the historical sequence of events contained in books 1–6, following the loose pattern of the maturation of the hero.

Landino's hero, however, is not the Everyman of Fulgentius

and Bernardus; he is a particularly gifted man working towards a full achievement of his traditional epithet, *pius*—a word that in Landino's reading comes to embrace the whole range of relation of fathers and sons, king and subject, mind and body, individual intelligence and eternal wisdom. Aeneas's goal is Italy, which Landino flatly equates with contemplation, and he struggles to free himself from the attractions of corporeal existence and to achieve the stability of the contemplative life. Landino differs slightly from his predecessors in his more rigorous attention to details of the text (he occasionally understands as the allegory of a passage what Bernardus would identify as only the overt moral) and in his interpretation of some of those details (Anchises, for example, he understands as sensuality because he is Aeneas's mortal parent, the father of his body). Also, his Platonizing of the text is distinctly Renaissance and much marked by the thought of his friend Marsilio Ficino (he identifies Aeneas's mother Venus with the angelic intelligence discussed in the *Symposium*). Yet the broad outlines of his interpretation still follow those of Fulgentius and Bernardus. Aeneas's descent into hell is still the descent of the mind *in sensualitatem* that it may gain knowledge of what ought to be sought and what to be avoided, and it is also the descent of the soul into the body. Misenus still remains, etymologically, false glory, and must be buried before the mind can free itself to pursue true knowledge. And however much Landino ignores the last six books, he still implicitly preserves Bernardus's and Fulgentius's mirroring structure in his explanation of the Sibyl's warning to Aeneas of the graver dangers yet before him: having passed through the storms of the active life, he must yet face the resurgence of memory and desire for those things which the life devoted to contemplation must put aside.

Landino makes three significant changes in the interpretative tradition: first, he raises his hero to the status of exceptional man, destined for glory; second, he focuses attention almost exclusively on Aeneas's journey and makes that central to his reading; and third, he explains the Dido episode, in accordance with his active-contemplative dialectic, not as the attraction of carnality but as the lure of the active, civic life which distracts man from his progress towards the true *summum bonum*, the contemplation and possession of wisdom. This last is completely consistent with

Landino's overall view of the *Aeneid* and with the positions taken by the participants in the discussions which form the first two books of the *Disputationes Camaldulenses:* the contemplative life is superior to and provides the norms for the active life. But the other two dramatically alter the nature of the epic poem and prepare the way for the kind of perception of epic that will culminate in the paragon hero of neoclassical prescriptive criticism and through him in the demise of formal verse epic itself. Despite this, we should not lose sight of how firmly located in the exegetical tradition Landino's reading of the *Aeneid* is. Epic for him is still inextricably tied up with notions of education, of knowledge, and of wisdom—however much he may alter the meanings of those words—and they are still bound to and culminate in the descent to hell.

This does not mean that notions about epic remain monolithic from classical times to the Renaissance. Far from it. What Fulgentius does to Virgil's poem in his commentary is already a major realignment of it, to Christianity if to nothing else. Bernardus extends those tendencies, and Landino modifies them even further, probably in a disastrous way, when he shifts so much of his emphasis in interpretation onto the journey itself that that portion of epic comes to seem the whole of it, and again, perhaps just as dangerously, when he construes Aeneas not as Bernardus's flawed Everyman but as the exceptional man who is destined for glory—glory being somewhat ambiguously allied to Christian beatitude. But even with these crucial changes, the broad outlines of the tradition have been preserved. The epic poem consistently dramatizes a descent which is paradoxically an ascent. It consistently presents the human mind, spirit, or soul—Man himself—descending into corporeal matter and coming to terms with it and, illuminated about his dual nature, at last freeing himself from the dominion of the grave clothes of the flesh. Epic is in this sense, in its more fundamental reality, the vehicle of the central myth of the West, the myth of consciousness, of the acquisition of new knowledge. The process depicted in the epic poem and the process enacted by the narrative itself is centroversion: the raising to consciousness of what had previously been latent, unknown, unappreciated. The recognition of this fact and the translation of it into terms accessible to their cultures are the major accomplishments of Fulgentius, Bernardus, and Landino; by their critical labors they extended the life of formal verse epic and made it a viable form for their times.

NOTES TO THE INTRODUCTION

1. Macrobius *Saturnalia* 5. 1. 18–20, trans. Percival Vaughan Davies (New York and London: Columbia University Press, 1969), p. 285.
2. Tasso, "Discourses on the Heroic Poem," trans. Allan H. Gilbert, in Allan H. Gilbert, *Literary Criticism: Plato to Dryden* (Detroit, Mich.: Wayne State University Press, 1962), pp. 500–501.
3. The phrase is E. R. Curtius's: see his *European Literature and the Latin Middle Ages*, trans. Willard R. Trask (New York: Pantheon, 1953), p. 443. His discussion of Macrobius has been especially useful to us.
4. Servius denies there is any such place as the *inferos* and posits that all Virgil says of the underworld is meant of life in this world, thus partially at least preparing the way for the later Christian allegorists of the descent. See J. W. Jones, Jr., "Allegorical Interpretation in Servius," *Classical Journal*, 56 (1961), 217–26.
5. John Dryden, "A Discourse concerning the Original and Progress of Satire," *Essays of John Dryden*, ed. W. P. Ker, 2 vols. (1900; reprint ed., New York: Russell and Russell, 1961), 2:36.
6. Fulgentius, *The Exposition of the Content of Virgil according to Moral Philosophy*, in *Fulgentius the Mythographer*, trans. and introd. Leslie George Whitbread (Columbus: Ohio State University Press, 1971), p. 122.
7. Ibid., p. 132.
8. Ibid., p. 125.
9. Ibid., pp. 123–24.
10. For important and illuminating assessments of Bernardus's place in the literature and learning of his times, see especially Brian Stock's *Myth and Science in the Twelfth Century: A Study of Bernard Silvester* (Princeton, N.J.: Princeton University Press, 1972) and Winthrop Wetherbee's *Platonism and Poetry in the Twelfth Century: The Literary Influence of the School of Chartres* (Princeton, N.J.: Princeton University Press, 1972) and his *The Cosmographia of Bernardus Silvestris: A Translation with Introduction and Notes* (New York and London: Columbia University Press, 1973).
11. Wetherbee remarks importantly on this similarity: see *Platonism and Poetry*, pp. 124–25.

12. Compare, for example, *The "Sphere" of Sacrabosco and its Commentators* ed. and trans. Lynn Thorndike (Chicago: University of Chicago Press, 1949), p. 123: "Be it understood that the 'first movement' means the movement of the *primum mobile*, that is, of the ninth sphere or last heaven, which movement is from east through west back to east again, which is also called 'rational motion' from resemblance to the rational motion in the microcosm, that is, in man, when thought goes from the Creator through creatures to the Creator and there rests."

13. The only modern edition of Landino's allegorization is the edition and translation of the last two books of the *Disputationes Camaldulenses* by Thomas H. Stahel: "Cristoforo Landino's Allegorization of the *Aeneid*: Books III and IV of the *Camaldolese Disputations*" (Ph.D. diss., The Johns Hopkins University, 1968). Some of our discussion of Landino draws on the introduction to this edition. A very full discussion of the nature of Renaissance allegoresis of Virgil can be found in Don Cameron Allen, "Undermeanings in Virgil's *Aeneid*," in *Mysteriously Meant: The Rediscovery of Pagan Symbolism and Allegorical Interpretation in the Renaissance* (Baltimore, Md.: Johns Hopkins University Press, 1970), pp. 135–62. As Allen there notes, an Italian edition of Virgil's works, first printed in 1576 and republished many times thereafter until at least 1710, served as an important means of disseminating, with elaborations, Landino's allegorization of the *Aeneid*. See *L'opere di Virgilio Mantoano, commentate . . . da Fabrini, Malatesta, e Venuti.*

A Note on the Translation

WE have used the critical edition of Julian Ward Jones and Elizabeth Frances Jones, *The Commentary on the First Six Books of the Aeneid of Vergil Commonly Attributed to Bernardus Silvestris* (Lincoln and London: University of Nebraska Press, 1977). This new edition is eminently superior to the earlier edition of Wilhelm Riedel, *Commentum Bernardi Silvestri super sex libros Eneidos Virgilii* (Greifswald: Julius Abel, 1924), which is based on only one, defective manuscript.

Keeping the needs of readers of translations in mind, we have in some ways diverged from the Joneses' edition. We have regularized proper names except those cited directly by Bernardus from whatever text (or texts) of the *Aeneid* he used, but we retain the medieval spelling of the catchwords as they appear in Bernardus's text. We have altered some syntax and frequently changed many past tenses to the historical present to conform with conventional English usage. Because Bernardus frequently comments word-by-word in Book 6, we have at times combined his comments into larger syntactic units. Finally, in Book 6, we have in some places altered the paragraphing. Line numbers in brackets refer to standard modern editions. In all of these changes our aim has been to provide as readable a text as possible without compromising the integrity of the *Commentary*.

We have not translated the continuation of the *Commentary* after Book 6, line 636 because (in agreement with the Joneses and most scholars) we believe it to be the work of a different author.

The notes have four major functions: to identify the sources of Bernardus's quotations (except where brief enough to cite parenthetically in the text), to provide additional explanation where necessary, to provide cross references within the text, and to set Bernardus's commentary within the larger context of medieval and Renaissance allegorizations of the *Aeneid*. Because both Fulgentius and Landino (like Bernardus) comment sequentially on the *Aeneid*, we omit specific line or page references, except in cases of direct quotation. This practice is especially necessary for Landino's commentary, of which there is no uniform or standard edition. References to classical texts give the standard line or section numbers of modern editions. Biblical references are to the Douay-Rheims translation, the English version closest to the Vulgate text which Bernardus used. We have omitted many of the analogues cited by the Joneses. Because we cite three works frequently in the notes, we use a short form for each:

Fulgentius Fulgentius, *The Exposition of the Content of Virgil according to Moral Philosophy (Expositio continentiae Virgilianae secundum philosophos moralis)*, in *Fulgentius The Mythographer*, translated, with introductions, by Leslie George Whitbread (Columbus: Ohio State University Press, 1971).

Commentary Macrobius, *Commentary on the Dream of Scipio (Commentarii in somnium Scipionis)*.

Consolation Boethius, *The Consolation of Philosophy (De consolatione philosophiae)*.

Unless otherwise noted, all translations are our own.

COMMENTARY ON
The First Six Books
of Virgil's *Aeneid*

Preface

WE hold that in the *Aeneid* Virgil has "the observance of twofold teaching," as indeed Macrobius says: "He taught the truth of philosophy, and he did not neglect poetic fiction."[1] Therefore, anyone who wishes to read the *Aeneid* as the nature of this work demands must first of all indicate the intention, the mode, and the objective of the work and then not fail to observe the double point of view of philosophy and poetic fiction in discussing these matters.

Because in our work we treat Virgil both as poet and as philosopher, we will briefly explain first the poet's intention, his mode of writing, and his objective in writing. He intends to set forth the fate of Aeneas and the other Trojans who, like Aeneas, endure the hardships of exile. Virgil does not write, however, the true version of the story, as does Dares Phrygius; rather, he extolls the deeds of Aeneas using poetic fictions so that he might earn the favor of Augustus. In his writing, Virgil, the greatest of the Latin poets, imitates Homer, the greatest of the Greek poets: for just as Homer speaks of the fall of Troy in the *Iliad* and of the exile of Ulysses in the *Odyssey*, so too does Virgil narrate the destruction of Troy in the second book of the *Aeneid* and the hardships of Aeneas in the remaining books.

We must note here that there is a double order of narration: natural and artificial. Natural order occurs when the narration follows temporal and historical sequence, because what is told occurs in the order that it happened, and thus what was done first is distinguished from what was done second and from what was done last. Lucan observes this order. In contrast, artificial order occurs when we artificially begin the narration in the middle and then return to the beginning. Terence uses this order, and so does Virgil in the *Aeneid*. It would be natural order if the narration first described the fall of Troy and then led the Trojans to Crete, from Crete to Sicily, and finally from Sicily to Libya.[2] But the narration first takes the Trojans to Dido and then introduces Aeneas, who recounts the fall of Troy and the other events which happened to him. We have thus far shown the intention and mode of the work, and now we consider its objective.

Some poets (such as the satirists) write for instruction; some (such as the comic playwrights) write for delight; and some (such as the historians) write for both. Horace speaks about this: "Poets aim either to benefit or to amuse or to utter words at once both pleasing and helpful to life" (*Art of Poetry* 333–34). The *Aeneid* gives pleasure because of verbal ornament, the figures of speech, and the diverse adventures and works of men which it describes. Indeed, anyone who imitates these matters diligently will attain the greatest skill in the art of writing, and he will also find in the narrative the greatest examples of and inspiration for pursuing virtue and avoiding vice. Thus, there is a double gain for the reader: the first is skill in composition which comes from imitation, and the second is the good sense to act properly which comes from the stimulus of examples. For instance, the labors of Aeneas are an example of patience; similarly, we are called to religion by Aeneas's piety toward Anchises and Ascanius, by his veneration of the gods and the oracles which he consults, by the sacrifices which he offers, and by the devotion and prayers which he utters. We are recalled from appetite for unlawful things by his immoderate love for Dido.

The function of a preface is simply to establish a friendly disposition in the reader or listener so that he may be attentive and be instructed. Even though many writers of prefaces investigate seven points, we believe that these three which we have considered are sufficient: the author's intention, which makes the reader teachable; his mode of writing, which makes the reader favorably disposed; and his objective, which makes the reader attentive.³ Let us now consider these matters with regard to philosophical truth. To the extent that he writes about the nature of human life, Virgil is a philosopher. His procedure is to describe allegorically by means of an integument what the human spirit does and endures while temporarily placed in the human body. Virgil uses natural order when writing about this, and thus he observes the double order of narration—as poet, the artificial order; as philosopher, the natural order.

The integument is a type of exposition which wraps the apprehension of truth in a fictional narrative, and thus it is also called an *involucrum*, a cover. One grasps the utility of this work, which is self-knowledge; it is very useful for man to know himself, as Macrobius says: "From the sky comes *nothis elitos*," that is, know yourself.⁴

We have thus far considered the intention, the mode, and objective according to the twofold instruction of the work; we now will consider the work book by book so that we can interpret the allegory of each of the twelve books.

Book 1

SUMMARY

IN the first book Juno comes to Aeolus. She gives her nymph Deiopea to him. Aeneas is tossed about by storms. He escapes with seven ships. Hidden under a cloud, he comes to Carthage; he sees his companions but does not speak with them until Venus removes the cloud. Aeneas is then entertained with a banquet and with songs from Iopas's harp. Dido welcomes Cupid in the likeness of Ascanius. Since all of these events pertain to man's first age, Virgil narrates them in the first book.[1]

INTERPRETATION

We have read that four children of Saturn and Ops escaped the teeth of their father when Saturn devoured all the others. The four are Jupiter, the god of all the others; Juno, the wife and sister of Jove and the goddess of birth; Neptune, the god of water; and Pluto, the god of Erebus. The children of Saturn and Ops (that is, of time and matter) are those material things which are brought forth in time into the world; time destroys all of these things except the four elements. The god of all earthly things is called Jupiter, that is, the superior fire which embraces all things and is higher than them. The god of water is called Neptune, since all waters proceed from the sea. The god of Erebus is called Pluto, that is, the earth, because the heaviness of the earth dominates the fallen world. Their sister is called Juno, that is, air, because material things derive from air. She is also called Jove's consort because air receives heat from fire and is subject to it. She is also called the goddess of birth because the young are conceived, formed, brought forth, and nourished by the heat and moisture of air. Thus she is called Juno, as if *novos iuvans*, "helping the young." She is called Lucina, as if *lucem natis prebens*, "giving light to the born."

We read that Aeolus is the god or king of winds who stirs up the sea with winds. By this we understand childbirth which is called Aeolus, as if *eonolus*, that is, the destruction of the real world,[2] since when a man is born, the world (that is, the life of the spirit) dies, as long as it is oppressed by the heaviness of the flesh, descends from its divinity, and assents to the passions of the flesh. This Aeolus stirs up winds, since a person's birth suffers disturbances of vices according to the constellations. Thus philosophy teaches that the birth of a child stirs up vices according to the constellations, that is, the powers of the stars. It calls "constellations" those powers which the stars have when they are ascendant in their houses, which are called *abisides*. Thus, if a child's birth occurs in the constellation of Saturn (that is, while that star is ascendant in Cancer and far from other stars which inhibit its nature), then the vices of torpor, of laziness, and of negligence result. If, however, the birth occurs in the constellation of Mars, then the vices of ire, madness, and temerity result; if in the constellation of Venus, lust. Thus, Aeolus (that is, birth) brings forth winds (that is, the excitement of vice). With these he attacks the sea, the human body which is a deep whirlpool of ebbing and flowing humors.

Deiopea is one of Juno's handmaids, more beautiful than the others. Although Phoebus and Aurora have fourteen daughters, Deiopea is closer to Juno even than Iris. We understand Juno's handmaidens, namely the concomitants of air, to be the natural properties and effects of air, that is, the qualities and varieties of storms. They wait upon Juno, and they are the aspects of air: lightness, mobility, heat, moisture, clearness, thinness, and respirability.[3] It is natural for air to be clear, unless it is condensed accidentally by the coldness of the water or the earth, because then the brightness of the sun cannot penetrate it. It is likewise natural for the air to be thin, delicate and imperceptible. In addition, it is respirable in the lower world; indeed, we are not able to breathe the air in higher regions because of its excessive thinness. But obviously one cannot breathe the fire of the highest regions, and thus no one can survive for long at a very high altitude. Juno sends this greatest handmaiden of hers to keep all creatures alive.

Now the other seven handmaidens of Juno are the seven storms of the air. We call them aerial storms either because air produces them or because they are produced in air. Three of these are adjuncts of Iris who always accompany her: first rain, second hail, third snow. We shall briefly look at the origin of these three. Heat, which is the divisive power of fire, breaks down the inferior moisture of solid things. The minute particles, that is, the drops, of this moisture rise because of their lightness, and if they are joined together by the force of wind or the strength of coldness, then they, made heavier by this conjunction, fall again as rain because of their weight. But if at any time the drops of moisture are joined together and made heavier and frozen by the power of cold, then hail falls. But if they are frozen while still minute particles, then snow falls.

During these storms it happens that a cloud faces the sun, and the cloud is in some places dense, in some more dense, and in some most dense; in some places pure, in some more pure, and in some most pure. When the sun shines on the cloud, where the cloud is most dense the rays are trapped as if in a glass, and they reflect a black color; where the cloud is less dense, a cerulean color; where even less dense, red; where pure, yellow; where more pure, green; where most pure, white. Thus, according to its greater purity, the cloud takes on colors closer to white; according to its greater density, the cloud takes on colors closer to black. Thus Iris (the rainbow) is nothing but a cloud facing the sun and taking shape in many ways from the rays of the sun. And therefore, since one of the storms we have already mentioned always accompanies Iris, they are called her handmaidens, that is, the attendants of this same Iris and the lesser handmaidens of Juno. Someone of these three handmaidens always accompanies Iris everywhere, and therefore Ovid says: "Iris, the messenger of Juno, clad in

Book 1   9

robes of many hues, draws up waters" (*Metamorphoses* 1. 270–71). Thus, Iris is the first of Juno's handmaidens to have her own handmaidens, the second is the whirlwind, the third is the comet, the fourth is lightning, the fifth is thunder, the sixth is smoke, and the seventh is earthquake. And so we have said that these tempests are aerial because they occur either in the air or by means of the air and thus are Juno's handmaidens. We have already spoken of Iris, and now let us consider the others.

Sometimes it happens that two winds from different parts of the world come together aloft and compress a cloud, and they condense it with violent force into a denser and longer form. It catches fire either because the rays of the sun have descended into it or because of its velocity, and at the same time the trapped violence of the winds pushes the cloud in the direction of least resistance, so that people think there is a wandering star or burning spear, and people call such figures whirlwinds, that is, heat. If indeed four opposing winds should compress that cloud (since they come from each part of the world), then the shape is round. In such an event, the whirlwind is believed to be a shooting star and is called a comet. And since among the four winds one will prevail, the comet speeds away from it in another direction. But since another wind resists the comet violently, the comet gives off a tail. Juno sends this handmaiden as a foretelling of the changes of kings, whence Lucan, "the hair of the foreboding star" (*Pharsalia* 1. 528–29), and Juvenal, "the comet threatening the king of Armenia" (*Satires* 6. 407). It is said that this sign frequently so terrified people that they deposed their kings, because the people believed that these phenomena occur as a result of the tyranny of kings. Because we shall speak about thunder and lightning later, we defer discussion of them. Juno similarly sends volcanic smoke and earth tremors. The body of the earth is similar to the human body. Just as in the human body there are passages for the humors (that is, the veins through which the blood flows and from which it pours out when a wound is inflicted), so too there are veins in the earth which are called cataracts, through which the water flows and from which it escapes if the earth is dug deeply. And likewise just as there are arteries in the human body through which the breath flows throughout the body, so too in the earth there are caverns through which the wind blows. If these caverns are large, they hold a great deal of air. When the force of this air encounters anything solid, it cannot break out while the solid object is in the way, nor, since it is mobile, can it stand still. There is a clash, and the repercussion from the encounter shakes the earth. The earth tremor will continue until the wind either draws back or breaks out with an eruption of the obstructing matter. And thus Juno causes earth tremors. Juno sends smoke in this way. If the caverns of the earth are narrow, the great power of the wind cannot enter them, and its lesser power cannot shake the earth. By repeatedly scraping along the ground and rubbing against the sulphurous veins of the earth, the wind generates fire, and so in volcanoes it brings forth smoke.

Thus the seven aerial natures and the seven tempests, and thus there are fourteen handmaidens of Juno. Clearness—the brilliance of the air which we call Deiopea—is the most beautiful of these. She is called Deiopea as if *demooipa*, that is, *communis oculus*, "the common eye," since because of brilliance each of us sees everything in common.[4]

What we have said thus far about Juno, Aeolus, and Deiopea should be sufficient, since both here and in other places in this book this is all the information that is necessary. From these interpretations one can understand why Juno should come to Aeolus and why she should give Deiopea to him. Juno comes to Aeolus since air initiates birth by heat and moisture. For just as cold and dryness retard by constriction and dessication (and for that reason melancholic women are very often sterile), so in contrast heat and moisture initiate birth by loosening and moistening. Thus Virgil admonishes the grooms to drive the mares when they are about to foal so that giving birth will be quicker and easier because of the moistening of sweat and the loosening from heat.[5] Juno sends Deiopea to Aeolus, that is, she lends her usual and customary brilliance to birth.

Aeneas is said to be the son of Anchises and Venus. Anchises means *celsa inhabitans*, "inhabiting the heavens"; we understand him to be the father of all who presides over all. We read that there are indeed two Venuses, one lawful, and the other the goddess of lust. The lawful Venus is the harmony of the world, that is, the even proportion of worldly things, which some call Astrea, and others call natural justice. This subsists in the elements, in the stars, in the seasons, in living beings. The shameless Venus, however, the goddess of lust, is carnal concupiscence which is the mother of all fornications.[6]

One must remember in this book as well as in other allegorical works that there are equivocations and multiple significations, and therefore one must interpret poetic fictions in diverse ways. For example, in Martianus's book one should interpret Jove sometimes as the superior fire, sometimes as a star, and even sometimes as the Creator himself; likewise, one should interpret Saturn in some places as the star, in other places as time; similarly, one should sometimes interpret Mercury as eloquence and sometimes as the star.[7] Hence, one must pay attention to the diverse aspects of the poetic fictions and the multiple interpretations in all allegorical matters if in fact the truth cannot be established by a single interpretation. This principle holds, therefore, in this work because the same name designates different natures, and conversely, different names designate the same nature, so that Apollo sometimes designates the sun, sometimes divine wisdom, and sometimes human wisdom; Jupiter sometimes designates fire and sometimes God; Venus sometimes designates the concupiscence of the flesh and sometimes the concord of the world (as we said above). Diverse names can signify the same thing (which is the definition of multivocation), as when both Jupiter and Anchises designate the Creator. Therefore, whenever you find Venus as the wife of Vulcan, the mother of Jocus and Cupid, interpret her as pleasure of the flesh, which is joined with natural heat and causes pleasure and copulation. But whenever you read that Venus and Anchises have a son Aeneas, interpret that Venus as the harmony of the world and Aeneas as the human spirit. Aeneas is so named as if *ennos demas*, that is, *habitator corporis*, "the inhabitant of the body," for *ennos* in Greek is *habitator* in Latin. Thus Juvenal calls Neptune *Ennosigeum*, that is, *habitatorem Sigei*, "the inhabitant of Sigeum" *(Satires* 10. 182). *Demas* (that is, *vinculum,* "chain") indeed means the body, because the body is the prison of the spirit.[8] Therefore Aeneas is the son of Venus and Anchises, since the human spirit comes from God through concord to live in the human body. We have said these things about Anchises, Aeneas, and Venus because in many places in this work we will find these interpretations necessary.

After Deiopea has been given to Aeolus, Aeneas is beset with dangers. The sea is understood as the human body, because drunkenness and desire (which are the waters) flow from it, and the turbulence of vice is in it, and there are channels for food and drink through it. According to this metaphor, we read that Venus was born from Saturn's genitals in the sea. For Saturn's genitals are the qualities of heat and moisture by which time creates things. Saturn's genitals are cast into the sea, since the excess of food and drink affects the body. The genitals, warmed by food in the body, produce lust, and it is therefore said that "without Ceres and Bacchus, Venus freezes."[9]

After Deiopea is given to Aeolus, Aeneas is cast about on the sea which we have been discussing—after the light of day has been given at birth (that is, after the child has been born), the spirit endures great oppression in the body because of frequent ingestions and eliminations. In man, heat naturally flourishes excessively, because it demands frequent ingestion and elimination of food and drink to resist its natural decrease and to nourish itself. Consequently, dense vapor, rising to the head and filling the arteries and natural cells of the brain impedes the powers of wit, reason, memory, and the natural strengths. Thus Aeneas and his companions are vexed by ocean swells; that is, the spirit and its powers are harassed by the ingestions and eliminations of the body. Moreover, he loses some of his companions for a time because reason and other abilities which he again acquires as he gets older and applies himself to study and learning are temporarily lost in infancy.[10]

Aeneas escapes with seven ships. We understand the seven ships to be seven desires bearing Aeneas and his companions away. Throughout the work we understand the ships as desires which draw us to different things. The first ship is the desire of seeing; the second, of hearing, the third, of tasting; the fourth, of smelling, the fifth, of touching; the sixth, of moving, the seventh, of being at rest. Indeed, the other ships, which he loses for a time and then regains, are the desires of discerning, of understanding, of restraining vices, and of pursuing virtue.

Cymothoë and Triton pull these seven ships "from the sharp cliff." Triton is the god of the sea, and Cymothoë is the goddess of the sea. Triton, as if *contritio*, "unhappiness," is vexation of the flesh. He is called the god of the sea since he dominates the body. He is said to blow a trumpet, since bodily vexation vents itself vocally in wailing, that is, weeping. For when an infant is hungry, thirsty, or cold, he weeps. *Cymothoë* means *ornata dea*, "adorned goddess." *Cema* means *ornatus*, "adorned"; and *theos* means *deus*, "god." Therefore *Cymothoë*, as if *Cematheos*, that is, *dea ornata leticia*, "goddess adorned with joy." She also blows a trumpet, that is, an outburst of laughter.

The sea cliff which hinders the ships is the heaviness and indolence of the flesh, which do not allow desires to fulfill themselves. Frequently a man wishes to go, see, hear, or do something, but indolence prevents him. Vexation or happiness excites desires, as when a man wishes to eat because he is hungry or to go to watch games because he is happy.

Hidden under a cloud, Aeneas comes to Carthage. Just as a cloud obscures light, so too does ignorance obscure wisdom. In ignorance he comes to Carthage, that is, to the new city of the world, the city which indeed has all inhabitants in itself. Dido, that is, passion, rules this city. This city is new to Aeneas because he has just been brought to it.

Aeneas "feasts his eyes on empty pictures." Because the world is then new to him and he is wrapped in a cloud (that is, in ignorance), he does not understand the nature of the world; therefore these please him, and he admires them. We understand his eyes as the senses, some of which are true and some false; just as there is a right eye and a left one, so too we know certain senses are true and others false. We understand the pictures to be temporal goods, which are called pictures because they are not good but seem so, and therefore Boethius calls them "images of true good."[11] And thus he fills his eyes (his senses) with pictures (that is, with worldly goods).

In this city he finds a woman ruling and the Carthaginians enslaved, because in this world such is the confusion that desire rules and virtues are oppressed. We understand the Carthaginians, brave and upright men, as virtues, and thus men serve and a woman rules. Therefore in divine books the world is called the city of Babylon, that is, the city of confusion.[12]

Hidden by a cloud, Aeneas sees his companions; they do not see him, nor does he speak with them. Those who accompany Aeneas are called his companions, just as the body and its members are the companions of the soul. For the spirit leads the members of the body wherever it wishes. He sees his companions but is not seen by them. For the spirit knows the body, but the body knows nothing of the spirit. He does not then talk with them, since he does not yet hold back the members from shameful acts or urge them to honest ones.

Venus removes the cloud. For pleasure, by urging the use of things, causes them to be known, and so she removes the cloud.

He is entertained with a banquet and Iopas's songs; he is led along with food and charmed by youthful babbling. For Iopas means *puerilis taciturnitas*, "youthful speechlessness," since however much noise he makes, he does not form even the most trivial word.[13]

He welcomes Cupid in Ascanius's shape. In the first age one has the desire for many things, to the degree that, although all new things please him, he does not know what he wants or whether it is reasonable. Aeneas feels his desire and therefore welcomes Cupid but does not recognize Cupid.[14]

In Ascanius's shape. Ascanius is the son of Aeneas and Creusa. Creusa is appetite, so named as if *creans usum*, "creating the use," that is, the power of the appetite for good, which is called the wife of Aeneas because it is naturally joined with the human spirit. For there is no spirit without its appetite. This appetite brings about the use of something, that is, habit. For when anything is desired for a good purpose, the labor by which it is achieved becomes a matter of habit or of desire. Therefore, appetite, that is, the desiring of the good, is the cause of habit, and Creusa is thus called. She is the mother of Ascanius. Ascanius is interpreted as if *aschalenos*, that is *sine gradatione*, "without gradation." *A* means *non*, "no," and *schalenos* means *gradatio*, "gradation." We understand that to be the mean: it is said to be without gradation because it neither descends to deficiency nor ascends to excess. There are in fact degrees of deficiency, for we are able to do less about something than we ought, and still less, and so on ad infinitum. In excess, too, the degrees are infinite: for we are able to do more than we ought about something, and still more, and so on ad infinitum. But there is no degree in the mean, for there is no mean if we are able to do more or less about something, and thus Ascanius is so named. The spirit generates this mean out of its appetite by desiring neither more nor less than is proper, and thus is Ascanius the son of Aeneas and Creusa. The shape of Ascanius is honorable, for by its shape a thing is known. If anything appears honorable, then the mean is part of its value. Cupid has this shape when Aeneas welcomes him. For Aeneas in his first age considers his desires to be honorable. Thus, if anyone cannot satisfy his desire, then he will weep bitterly, as if something were unjustly denied him. Thus far, in the first book, the first age—infancy—is depicted.

Book 2

    Conticuere omnes, etc. In the second book Virgil describes the nature of the second age—childhood. Infancy is that first part of human life, which extends from birth to the time when a man naturally speaks. Childhood—the second part of human life—begins when a person comes under the discipline of instruction and continues until he leaves that custody. Therefore *infantia,* "infancy," is so called from the combination of *in* and *for, faris,* "not to speak"; *pueritia,* "childhood," is from *pure,* that is, *custodia,* "wardship." This is the greatest difference between infancy and childhood, because children speak, but infants are not able to speak naturally. Therefore, nothing else is allegorically represented in this second book except the beginning of speech and the ability to speak. Dido's persuading Aeneas to tell of his history shows nothing else except that desire wishing to be manifested urges him to bring forth words; and, in satisfying that desire, he breaks forth in speech. And since speech is sometimes true and sometimes false, the mixture of the truth of history and the falsity of fables in the narration follows this same pattern. The Greek destruction of Troy is history, but Aeneas's honesty is fiction for Dares Phrygius narrates that Aeneas betrayed his city.[1]

Book 3

Postquam res Asie et cetera. The nature of adolescence is expressed in the third book.[1] But so that we can interpret the allegory of this book later, we will first give the narrative briefly.

SUMMARY

After the burning of his city, Aeneas goes to Antandros, then to Thrace, Delos, Crete and the Strophades; he then sees the land of the Cyclops, and, being warned by Achaemenides, he also sees Polyphemus, whose eye Ulysses had put out at the time when he abandoned Achaemenides there. Aeneas buries his father in the seaport of Drepanum.

INTERPRETATION

Aeneas's city is the human body, in which the human spirit lives and rules, and therefore it is called his city. And again just as there are four types of dwellings in the city and the four orders of men living in these dwellings, so too in the human body there are four dwellings and four powers living in them.[2] The first dwelling in the city is the citadel, which the wise men inhabit: so too in the body the first and most distinguished dwelling and high fortress of the body is the head, in which wisdom dwells, and in the head are the instruments of the senses and the three chambers of wit, reason, and memory. The second dwelling place in the city belongs to the soldiers: so too the second dwelling place in the body is the seat of spirit in the heart, just as indeed that second place in the city is the dwelling place of the men of spirit. The third dwelling place in the city is the home of the men of desire: so too the third in the body is the seat of desire, which indeed is the loins. In the outskirts of the city are the suburbs, the homes of the farmers: so too at the extremities of the body are the hands and feet which produce action. And therefore the body is said to be a city. The burning of this city is the natural heat of the first age; having left that behind, Aeneas comes to Antandros. The Greek word *andros* means *vir*, "man," in Latin, whence *Evander* is *bonus vir*, "the good man," and *Andreas* is "the virile man." Indeed, *anti* means *contra*, "against." Thus, *Anthandros* means *contrarium virilitatis*, "the opposite of manliness." Manliness is thus properly called constancy, as if *viri qualitas*, "the quality of a man." This quality is naturally proper to men, and neither the child nor the youth nor the old man (who has returned to the nature of childhood) has this natural constancy. For Horace says about a child that "he flies into a passion and as lightly puts it aside, and he changes by the hour" (*Art of Poetry* 159–60). Concerning youth: he is "quick to discard his desires" (*Art of Poetry* 165). And Horace also describes what the constancy of man should be: "He fears having done what he might soon struggle to change" (*Art of Poetry* 168). Thus manliness (that is, the quality of a man) is constancy. Whence also the mathematicians say that the odd number is the number of man, as if men have the nature of indivisibility, that is, of constancy. Now Antandros (that is, the opposite of manliness) is inconstancy. This indeed is the first vice of adolescence. Because adolescents have not had use or experience of things, therefore they, desiring something, think it to be the best thing and cling to it; but when they do not find it to be what they thought it to be, they then turn immediately to something else. In contrast, men, because they recognize things from experience, therefore have stability concerning the things to which they adhere. And thus Aeneas comes to Antandros from the burning of the city; that is, from the natural heat of the first age which burns the body, he comes to the inconstancy of adolescence.

But since in the same place it says that the ships were crafted from the wood of Ida, we therefore must discuss this.

Book 3

We have said that Aeneas's ships are desires leading Aeneas and his companions (that is, the spirit and its powers) to diverse objectives; these were in Antandros, since diverse and infinite desires arise in inconstancy. For constant persons remain constant for as long as they wish, but inconstant persons sometimes do one thing, then another, and then something else, because, as Horace says, "they cannot endure for an hour liking the same things" (*Epistles* 1. 1. 82). Concerning inconstancy, Horace again says, "What he sought, he spurns; he repeats what he recently rejected; he tears down and builds up; he changes squares to circles."[3] Thus the fleet (that is, multitudes of desires) assembles in Antandros.

Ida is the grove of the Trojan city from which the ships are made. *Ida* means *pulchritudo*, "beauty," whence *Alcides* means *fortis et pulcher*, "strong and beautiful," and *Ganymede* is called *Ideus*, that is, "beautiful." But this grove is called the grove of the city, since the beauty of shape outwardly disguises the body, lest interior foulness appear. Indeed, the ships are made from the wood of Ida, since from the beauty of things comes the desire to seek them.[4]

Aeneas travels to Thrace. Thrace, which we properly understand as avarice, had the most avaricious king and inhabitants, and one reads a warning about avarice in this book: "*Fuge litus avarum,*" "Flee the shores of greed." He travels from Antandros to Thrace, that is, from inconstancy to avarice. Thus Horace, after he reproaches inconstancy in the first of the satires, then turns to avarice (*Satires* 1. 1. 1–40). Indeed, one proceeds from inconstancy to avarice in this manner: after surveying diverse things through inconstancy and trying everything, it seems that all temporal things can be had by riches, since "money gives birth and beauty and power, and Persuasion and Venus grace the man who is well off."[5] And therefore such a man is obsessed with being rich, and he so eagerly searches after money that he chooses it above everything else. Thus Aeneas travels from Antandros to Thrace.

He discovers Polymnestor reigning and Polydorus buried. *Polis* in Greek means *multum*, "much," in Latin, and *metros* means *mensura*, "measure." Whence Polymnestor, as if *polimetros*, that is, *plurium mensura*, "the measure of more things"—the heap of money which the greedy person wishes to count exactly for himself. This rules in avarice since it compels the greedy to heap up more for themselves by saying, "Be active and get rich." And so the greedy person slavishly devotes himself to heaping up much money or to increasing it, since "ardent trader that you are, you rush to the farthest Indies." Or he devotes himself to preserving it with great reverence, and for that reason Horace condemns him: "You have heaped up treasure from everywhere, and when you sleep you covet it, but you fear to touch it, as if it were sacred."[6] And so Polymnestor is king.

Polydorus means *multa amaritudo*, "great bitterness." For *doris* in Greek means *amaritudo*, "bitterness," in Latin. Thus in fables one reads that Doris is a goddess of the sea, since bitterness is dominant in seawater. Virgil gives this interpretation in saying, "Let not the bitter sea mingle with pure water" (*Eclogues* 10. 5). Thus Polydorus is buried in Thrace because there is great bitterness involved in avarice—for what is more bitter than the greedy person, because he "seeks wealth yet the wretch shrinks from his gains and fears to use them," and because "he manages everything fearfully and coldly," and because "love of money increases as the money increases," and because "the greedy person is always busy"?[7] Now Polydorus banishes Aeneas from Thrace, because the bitterness and effort of seeking and preserving money often deter the pursuit of money. And the rational spirit, seeing the bitterness of such anxiety in the greedy person, renounces and rejects the filthy life of avarice, saying, "Now, now, boy, baste the cabbages with expensive oil. Let my holiday dinner be made from nettles and a smoked hog's jowl with a split ear."[8]

Aeneas travels to Delos. Delos means *claritas*, "brightness," whence *Sol Delius* is rendered *clarus*, "bright." Understand this to be the honest life which is called Delos (that is, *claritas*, "brightness"), because there is nothing brighter in this life. And therefore, to anyone asking what should be the greatest good in life, respond "virtue." Apollo is worshipped there, since in the virtuous life wisdom is served. For he who lives virtuously does everything wisdom suggests. Anius, "the king and priest of Phoebus," reigns there. He is called Anius as if *aneos*, that is, *sine novitate*, "without novelty"; *a* means *sine*, "without," and *neos* means *novum*, "new." Thus also Neoptolemus, which means *novus miles*, "the new soldier," and *neomenia*, which means *nova luna*, "the new moon." Anius is indeed called wise. To the wise man who has had the use and experience of things, nothing new happens.[9] He is king and priest because he interprets divine theology and rules human affairs.

From Thrace they come to Delos, because Aeneas approaches virtue after casting off the filth of avarice. Anius entertains Aeneas at a banquet, since the wise man feeds the rational spirit with learning.

Aeneas is admonished by Apollo "to seek his ancient mother." The two ancient mothers, that is, the two regions of Crete and Italy, are the two origins of Aeneas, the nature of the body and the nature of the spirit. We understand Crete as corporeal nature, which is the certain beginning of Aeneas's temporal life. And, ironically, Crete is so named as if *cresis theos*, that is, *iudicium divinum*, "divine judgment." For carnal nature judges badly about divine matters whenever it values divinity less than temporal things. We understand Italy (which is interpreted as *incrementum*, "growth") as divine nature, which is rationality, immortality, virtue, and knowledge. Aeneas is commanded to seek these by Apollo, that is, by wisdom, for wisdom admonishes him to love the divine. But Aeneas misunderstands the oracle, and when he is commanded to go to Italy, he seeks Crete. He errs in Apollo's oracle thus: wisdom asks man, as one can read in Boethius (*Consolation*, bk. 2, prose 4, 1. 23), whether anything is valuable in itself. When one responds "very little," he is commanded to seek beatitude in himself. He who interprets "in himself" to mean "in the nature of the body" and thinks that to mean "the nature of the spirit" descends completely into pleasures of the flesh.[10] And thus Aeneas comes to Crete when he is ordered to go to Italy. But since he cannot rule there, he is ordered by the gods which he carries with him to leave. For as long as the spirit seeks its good in the nature of the flesh, it will not rule, but indeed serve both good and evil equally. Thus knowledge and virtues (which the divine mind carries with itself) warn him to flee the flesh.

Aeneas comes to the Strophades. *Stropha* means *conversio*, "turning," and *idor* means *aqua*, "water"; therefore, *ydromantia* means "divination in water." Thus *Strophades* (that is, *aquarum conversiones*, "the churning of the waters") are called islands since they churn up the water in whirlpools. We interpret these as the churnings of vicious men, for we interpret the waters as vices, which are Aeneas's shipwrecks. They are called islands, that is, they are placed *in salo*, in the ocean of this life. As long as he turns towards Italy from Crete, Aeneas is forced by storms towards the islands. For as long as he turns from the nature of the flesh toward the spirit, he is carried back by storms (that is, by the rushing excitements of the flesh) to vice. Thus, if a lecherous person attempts to come to purity of life, the flesh becomes stirred up and forces him to return to lechery. This is an example of such a commotion: "Think of how arduous the celibate life is, and think of how much pleasure there is in the flesh." By such a thought one is forced back into lechery. And thus as long as Aeneas turns away from Crete towards Italy, he is forced by storms towards the Strophades. In the sixth book we will talk about the Harpies which he finds there.

Aeneas sees the Cyclops. The Cyclops is so called as if *cyclopolis*, that is, *circulorum pluralitas*, "a multitude of circles," which we understand to be the multitude of aimless wanderings which adolescents endure.[11] He sees Polyphemus, whom Ulysses had blinded, and Achaemenides, whom Ulysses had abandoned there.

Ulysses beached his fleet on an island where he found Circe, the daughter of the Sun, who metamorphosed his companions with her potion, but he thwarted her by the counsel of Mercury and thus remained unchanged. Again by the counsel of Mercury, he fled Aetna and beached his fleet on an island where he discovered the one-eyed Polyphemus, whom he blinded to avenge his companions whom Polyphemus had devoured, and there he abandoned Achaemenides. Ulysses is so named as if *olonsenos*, that is, *sensus omnium*, "knowledge of everything," that is, *sapiens,* "wise," because he has experience of everything. He beached his fleet (that is, his desire) on the island. That land is called *insula,* "island", as if *in salo posita,* "placed in the sea," because it is completely surrounded by the ocean. On the island the ruler is Circe, that is, earthly wealth, which is called *circes,* "circle," as if *cirocrisis,* that is, *iudicium manuum,* "judgment by the hands," since earthly wealth is judged according to the manual labor it requires.[12] Circe is called the daughter of the sun because all wealth is born from his seed, that is, from the heat of the sun acting on the earth. She prepares potions from herbs (that is, the pleasures derived from temporal goods) by which Ulysses's companions (that is, senseless people who are the companions of the wise man) are changed into beasts. A man becomes a beast when he (who should naturally be rational and immortal because of his soul) becomes irrational and mortal because of excessive delight in temporal things. For who is more bestial than he who fits the definition of a beast? Who is more bestial than he who has the nature of a beast and nothing more than the form of a man? Ulysses's companions are changed into diverse kinds of beasts: swine, lions, dogs, wolves. Boethius clearly explains this: "If one sinks to foul and filthy pleasure, he shall be considered a swine; the one who is moved by anger is thought to have the soul of a lion; he who uses the language of quarrelsome people has a dog's bark; the secret schemer rejoices in his fraudulent theft, and he follows the habits of little foxes (*Consolation,* bk. 4, prose 3. 17–25). But Ulysses, rejecting pleasures, remains rational. In the fourth book we shall talk about Mercury, by whose counsel this happened.

After he has fled this island, Aeneas comes to Aetna. Aetna is the volcano situated high above the sea. The mountain signifies puffed-up pride. Because the mountain is filled inside with flames and consumed by them and because it burns up the surrounding area with them, it signifies that this interior pride, stirred up by the heat of anger, is consumed by its own heat and that men outside are afflicted by the same heat. Polyphemus is on this mountain. We understand Polyphemus (as if *polimunta femum,* that is, *perdentem famam,* "losing fame") to be the proud person.[13] For no one is of such virtue that he will not justly lose the fame of his virtue as soon as he is proud of it. Polyphemus is one-eyed. Men ought to have two eyes, that is, consideration of the eternal and of the temporal. The proud man however, considers only the temporal. Polyphemus devours Ulysses's companions when he draws these senseless men to himself. His eye is put out with a sharp stick when excessive consideration of and attention to the temporal is castigated by a sharp rebuke.

Achaemenides is so called as if *acheremenes*, that is, *sine gaudio et hilaritate*, "without joy and cheerfulness," and that condition is melancholy; after Ulysses had blinded Polyphemus, he abandoned Achaemenides. Having come to Aetna, Aeneas rescues Achaemenides—the spirit of the adolescent coming to pride becomes melancholic. He grieves because something stands in his way, since "he denies that laws are made for him, nor will he take up arms" (Horace *Art of Poetry* 122).

Aeneas buries his father in Drepanum. *Drepanum* (as if *drimus pes*) means *acerbitas puerilis*, "childish acerbity," the anger which most of all besets youths because of their excessive fervor. Aeneas buries his father in anger when God is given over to oblivion.[14] For the angry are almost apostates. The grave is a kind of oblivion.

Book 4

SUMMARY

At regina, etc: In the fourth book Virgil allegorically expresses the nature of young manhood. We first give a summary of the narrative, and then the interpretation of it.

Having buried his father, Aeneas goes hunting. Driven by storms into a cave, he dallies with Dido and there commits adultery. Receiving Mercury's counsel, he abandons this disgraceful way of life. Having been abandoned, Dido burns herself to ashes and dies.

INTERPRETATION

By direct and allegorical narration Virgil describes the nature of young manhood. When Aeneas goes hunting after burying his father, it signifies that the person oblivious of his creator is engaged in hunting and other vain endeavors which pertain to young manhood, as one reads in Horce: "The beardless youth, away from his guardian, rejoices in horses, dogs, and the grass of the playing field."[1] Aeneas is driven to a cave by storms and rain, that is, he is led to impurity of the flesh and of desire by excitement of the flesh and by the abundance of humors coming from a superfluity of food and drink. This impurity of the flesh is called a cave, since it beclouds the clarity of mind and of discretion. The abundance of humors from food and drink leads to impurity of passion in the following way. In digestion there are four humors: liquid, steam, foam, and sediment. After the humors of food and drink have been digested in the cauldron of the stomach, steam is then given off, and (as the nature of lightness demands) it ascends, and, having ascended and been collected in the arteries, it becomes less dense, moves to the brain, and produces the living powers. The liquid is condensed in the members of the body. The sediment is emitted by the lower passages through defecation, and the foam is emitted partially in sweat and partially through the sense openings. But when there is too great an abundance of foam (which happens in gluttonous eating and drinking), then it is emitted through the male member, which is nearest to and below the stomach, having first been converted into sperm, that is, the male seed, for the stomach is cleared out through the nearby and lower member. Thus one reads that Venus is born of sea foam and is therefore called *afroden*.

Thus the rain forces Aeneas to the cave. He is united with Dido and remains with her for a while. The public disgrace of a bad reputation does not check him, because a young man, having been snared by passion, does not know "what is beautiful, what is disgraceful, what is useful, or anything else" (Horace *Epistles* 1. 2. 3). But after long waywardness he is warned by Mercury to leave.

You should interpret Mercury sometimes as a star and sometimes as eloquence: he is a star in that fable in which Venus commits adultery with Mercury, by which you understand those stars in the ascendant joining their forces; Mercury is eloquence when he seeks marriage with Philology.[2] For eloquence without wisdom is of little help, and indeed it is often harmful.[3] He is therefore depicted as a bird or dog, because speech runs about quickly. He is said to carry a wand with which he divides serpents, because he has the explanation by which he separates quarrelers and the purveyors of poisonous words. He is said to be patron of robbery because he deceives the souls of listeners. He is said to control merchants, since those selling goods further themselves with eloquence. Whence he is called Mercury, as if *mercatorum kirios*, that is, "the god of merchants," or as if *medius discurrens*, "running in the center," or as if *mercatorum cura*, "the guardian of merchants," or as if *mentium currus*, "the activity of the mind," because he reveals carefully contrived matters. And thus he is also called Hermes, that is, *interpres*, "explanation." For *Hermenia* is *interpretatio*, "interpretation."

Book 4   27

Mercury warns and censures Aeneas because he finds him ignoring useful endeavor, for Aeneas is "the tardy provider of the useful," and "wasteful of money" (Horace *Art of Poetry* 164). With a speech of certain censure, Mercury chides Aeneas, who leaves Dido and puts passion aside. Having been abandoned, Dido dies, and, burned to ashes, she passes away. For abandoned passion ceases and, consumed by the heat of manliness, goes to ashes, that is, to solitary thoughts.[4]

Book 5

SUMMARY
Interea, et cetera. In the fifth book Virgil begins the age of manhood. The story tells that Aeneas celebrated games. The ships are burned. Aeneas is instructed to descend to the underworld to see his father. Palinurus dies.

INTERPRETATION
After Aeneas rejects Dido, he celebrates four games in honor of his father; having abandoned the lust of youth, Aeneas makes a sacrifice to God by the exercise of four virtues in his time of manhood. We understand the control of the ships to be temperance, which is the moderator of all desires. The boat race comes first, since in pursuing virtue one must first have moderation. For moderation overcomes vice, and thus it necessarily precedes the other virtues. Temperance is the dominance of reason over desire and over the other improper movements of the spirit. Interpret the boxing match in which they bear heavy weights as fortitude, by which one endures the burden of labor, for fortitude is the considered undertaking of dangers and the endurance of labor. Interpret the footrace and horserace, in which one notes the speed of men and horses, as prudence, by which the movement and instability of mutable things are known. So too in a race, some flee and some pursue, and thus prudence discerns what should be followed and what should be fled, for prudence is the recognition of both the good and the bad. Interpret the archery contest (in which arrows are shot afar) as justice, by which evildoers are removed to a

Book 5

distance, for justice is the virtue preserved for the common good and which lends its dignity to the common good.[1]

The ships are burned. While these games are going on, the Trojan women at the urging of Iris (who was in the shape of Beroë) burned the ships, because while the spirit is exercised in virtue, the frailties of the flesh (which are the Trojan women) will dare in the heat of passion to violate the society and friendship of Aeneas, thus frustrating honest desires which wish to bring them to Italy, that is, to growth.[2]

They do this at Iris's persuasion. Iris, who is multicolored and placed opposite to the sun, figures the senses, which are distinguished by their diverse species and powers and are contrary to reason. The senses have the power to perceive form, color, bitterness, sweetness, roughness, softness, denseness, thinness, and the harmony or discord of sounds. The senses are found to be contrary to reason in this way: just as you will read in Boethius, reason enhances the universal, but the senses seize a single instance (*Consolation*, bk. 5, prose 4. 28–29). Thus we understand Iris, who is multicolored and set opposite the sun, to be the multiplex senses set contrary to reason. In the *Timaeus* Plato tells what happens when sense is placed against reason: "The opposing natures resist the condensing and joining of the two modes."[3] Honest desires are corrupted by the persuasion of sense, because sense urges us only to things perceptible by the senses.

Iris appears in the likeness of Beroë. *Beroe* means *ordo veritatis*, "the order of truth,"[4] which is reason, which recognizes the true order of things since it judges God to be first, angels second, man third, brute animals fourth, living but insensate bodies (such as plants and trees) fifth, and inanimate things last. Sense masquerades as reason when it urges the burning of the ships, since it is thought to be rational although it is not rational.

Anchises' image instructs Aeneas to descend to the underworld to see him there; that is, Aeneas is instructed by a certain mental image coming from the Creator. For he is unable to have perfect thought, since God is not circumscribed by thought. He is admonished thus: to descend to earthly things through thought, and there he will see his father, because, although God dwells on high, one can have knowledge of the Creator nonetheless by comparing things of the world and recognizing their frailty. And therefore Aeneas is commanded to seek his father in the underworld, although the Father dwells in the heavens. In the sixth book we shall speak about the underworld and the descent into it.

Then Palinurus the helmsman dies. Palinurus is so called as if *palans noron*, that is, *errabundus visus*, "wandering vision."[5] Formerly he led Aeneas's fleet, that is, his desires; but when Aeneas is ordered to see his father, Palinurus dies, that is, wandering vision passes away.

Book 6

Sic fatur, etc: Since in this sixth book the narrative concerns Aeneas's descent into the underworld, we shall therefore consider first the descent and the places of the underworld; and since Virgil declares philosophic truth more profoundly in this book, we shall not only give a summary of the book, but we shall also spend more time interpreting individual words in it.

Before philosophy grew to a state of vigor, the professors of theology denied that the lower regions were anything except human bodies; indeed, they called the lower regions bodies because they had discovered nothing else lower among things. For, of that which exists, part is spirit, part is body, and part is the accidents of spirit or body. Indeed, the body is quite obviously lower than the spirit, since the spirit is immortal, rational, and indivisible, but the body is mortal, irrational, and divisible. Again, the spirit rules, and the body is ruled. The body is also lower than accidents, since they are incorporeal, and as Boethius says, contain their own immutable substance (*On Arithmetic* 1. 1). Therefore the body is lower than the spirit and accidents. Again, some bodily things are celestial, some are fallen. But who cannot see that those fallen things (which are dissoluble) are lower in station as much as in nature? The fallen things are those of men, of beasts, of plants, of trees, or of inanimate objects. Indeed, the human is lower than other things: than beasts, since the corporeal powers of beasts are greater than those in a human. For, as Boethius says, we shall not excel the elephants in bulk, the bulls in power, and the tigers in speed (*Consolation,* bk. 3, prose 8. 7). Likewise, the human body is lower than trees, because if a tree is damaged, it again becomes green and puts forth its branches. The human body is also lower than inanimate things. For among inanimate things what is more fragile than glass?—but the human body is inferior to it: the human body can perish by violent collision and sickness and old age, but glass can be destroyed by violent collision but not by sickness or old age. And, therefore, since nothing is lower than the human body, it is called *infernum*, the lower region. And because we also read that souls are forcibly held in the lower regions as if in spiritual prisons, people thus say that souls suffer the same thing in the body through vice.[1]

Four rivers are designated in the infernal regions: Phlegethon, the fires of the angry; Lethe, the oblivion of the mind forgetful of the majesty of its own divinity; Styx, hatred; and Acheron, sorrow.[2]

It is indeed true that these regions are infernal, but it is false that these are the only ones. Indeed, some people divide the world into two parts: inferior and superior. The superior part—*aplanen*—is called *paradisus* in Greek and in Latin *ortus*, "the origin," since things originate (*oriuntur*) from it; and it is called *Eden* in Hebrew, which in Latin we call *delicie*, "delights," because it is well known that the delights of souls are placed there. Indeed, that which is below *aplanen* (that is, lower), namely that fallen and lower region, people call *inferos*, the underworld.[3] Explaining in sequence, we shall teach how there might be in that region what we allegorically read to be in the underworld.

The descent to the underworld is fourfold: the first is natural, the second is virtuous, the third is sinful, the fourth is artificial.[4] The natural descent is the birth of man: for by it the soul naturally enters this fallen region and thus descends to the underworld and thus recedes from its divinity and gradually declines into vice and assents to pleasures of the flesh; this is common to everybody. The second descent is through virtue, and it occurs when any wise person descends to mundane things through meditation, not so that he may put his desire in them, but so that, having recognized their frailty, he may thoroughly turn from the rejected things to the invisible things and acknowledge more clearly in thought the Creator of creatures. In this manner, Orpheus and Hercules, who are considered wise men, descended. The third is the descent of vice, which is common and

Book 6

by which one falls to temporal things, places his whole desire in them, serves them with his whole mind, and does not turn away from them at all. We read that Eurydice descended in this way. Her descent, however, is irreversible. The fourth descent is through artifice, when a sorcerer by necromantic operation seeks through execrable sacrifice a conference with demons and consults them about future life.

The second and fourth descents are therefore especially noted in this book. For, according to the narrative, Aeneas descended to the underworld following the method of the last type of descent, and he sacrificed Misenus to the demons, and he sought a conference with the Sibyl, the Cumaean prophetess, and he inquired about the events of the future.[5] We shall now explain the second type of descent in terms of its fictional description in the narrative. First we shall set forth the narrative and then consider the allegorical foundation of it.

After the loss of Palinurus, Aeneas takes up the rudder and brings the ships to the grove of Trivia and to the golden roofs. He then sends Achates to the Sibyl, and he returns with her.

The interpretation: Having abandoned wandering vision, the rational spirit begins to rule its desire with reason (which is the rudder) by restraining desire from certain things and directing it to others. Aeneas then brings the fleet to the grove of Trivia, that is, he turns his will to the study of eloquence, the science which instructs its reader in the decorous utterance of thoughts. This is called *Trivia* since we come to it by three ways (*tribus viis*), that is, by three arts. In order to have perfect eloquence one must first know how to speak without solecism and barbarism, and this is attained through grammar. It is then necessary to know what to prove or disprove in speech, and this comes about through dialectic. Then it is necessary to know whether to persuade or dissuade: for listeners are able to know something by grammatical speech and to be certain about it by logical testing but still not desire it; therefore, rhetorical persuasion is necessary. And thus grammar is the beginning of eloquence, dialectic is its advancement, and rhetoric is its perfection; therefore, eloquence is called *Trivia*. The groves in which it dwells are those arts or books in which the science is taught. The golden roofs (*aurea tecta*) are the four mathematical arts in which philosophy (which is known by the ear, *aurum*) is contained.⁶ Aeneas's ship is drawn to these, that is, he applies his will first to grammar and then to the others in their order.

Achates (as if *a chere ethis*) is interpreted as *tristis consuetudo*, "sorrowful habit." For *a* means *sine*, "without"; *chere* means *leticia*, "joy"; *ethis* means *mos* or *consuetudo*, "custom" or "habit." This indeed is study, because study is a painstaking habit.⁷ Whence also it is defined: "Study is the vigorous and assiduous application of the spirit to doing something with the greatest desire."⁸ For what else is assiduity but habit? What else is vigor but painstaking? The Sibyl is indeed so called as if *scibule*, that is, *divinum consilium*, "divine counsel," which we take to be understanding, which is called counsel: by it man consults with himself. It is called divine because understanding is nothing else than the comprehension of divine matters.⁹ Having been sent, Achates brings the Sibyl back through the groves, since study exercised in the arts brings forth understanding.

Having taken care of these matters, let us return to the narrative.

[1] *Lacrimans:* Aeneas weeps for the loss of Palinurus. Since Aeneas was accustomed to obey his wandering vision and since habit is like a second nature, he therefore does not easily endure its withdrawal. Since his vision was pleasing to him, losing it saddens him. *Classi:* the multitude of ships, that is, desires. *Habenas:* the controls are instruments which at times are slackened and at times tightened; therefore, the rudder of the ship is reason, by which desire is governed. Aeneas has controls which recall the will from illicit things (that is, the ship from dangers) and direct it to honest things (and thus brings the ship to port).

[2] *Tandem*, after lengthy labors. *Euboicis:* Euboea is a region having many cities, among which is the city of the Cumaeans wherein the Sibyl dwells. *Euboea* means *bonus sonus*, "a good sound"; for *eu* means *bonum*, "good"; *boos* means *sonus*, "sound"; hence, *boare* means *sonare*, "to make a sound." This is knowledge, for knowledge is the comprehension of the knowable. There are four parts to this: wisdom, eloquence, poetics, and mechanics. Let us speak about the nature of wisdom and eloquence and about the parts of the others.¹⁰ Mechanics is the knowledge of human works connected with corporeal needs. There are seven parts to

it: weaving, armament, navigation, hunting, agriculture, theatrics, and medicine. Poetics is the knowledge of poets and has two parts—verse and prose. Thus every single art or species of knowledge is one of the cities of Euboea. The city of the Cumaeans (*Cumarum*) is in Euboea. *Cume* in Greek means *honeste mansiones*, "honest dwellings," in Latin. These are the philosophical arts, which are called dwellings, since the Sibyl is in them; that is, if anyone practices them, he uses understanding. They are called honest to differentiate them from mechanical arts, which are called *mecanice*, that is, *adulterine*, "forged."

[3–6] *Obtendunt pelago proras:* their desires are opposed to the passion of the flesh and the excitement of temporal things. *Tum dente tenaci:* since Virgil said that Aeneas and his companions, that is, the spirit and the spiritual desires, are opposed to the passion of the flesh and excitement of temporal things. And it is most difficult to show how they are able to do this with their ships, but Virgil narrates thus: they are able to turn the prows to the beach since "the anchor (*anchora*) holds the ship fast." We interpret the anchor here to be the same thing as in Boethius: "The anchors hold fast" (*Consolation*, bk. 2, prose 4. 9). Indeed, in both works we interpret the anchor as hope.[11] Hope is the expectation of future good and is properly designated by the anchor, because, just as that instrument does not allow the ship to drift, so hope does not permit desire to vacillate. Indeed it is said, "Good hope gives strength."[12] *Fundabat naves:* he makes desires stable. For when a man expects future reward, he sweats in his labors more constantly. *Dente tenaci:* with sure hope of reward. *Litora:* leaving the ocean and coming to port are the departure from passion of the flesh and from the excitement of temporal things and the beginning of study, and this is called the shore. *Curve:* inclined and disposed. *Puppes:* "the helms" are everywhere to be taken as desires. Note the order: first the ships are turned around from the sea, and then they are beached, since the desires are first to be counterposed to the fleshly passions and then set to the beginnings of study.[13] *Manus . . . ardens:* the multitude of youths manfully and bravely working in the fervor of virtue. *Litus:* the beginning of studying. *Hesperium:* clear. Hesper is the clearest star, of such brightness (as Martianus says) that its rays are more brilliant than those of any other heavenly body, except the sun or moon.[14] If on a clear night you do not immediately see the moon, which by its brightness dulls the brightness of Hesper, then that star casts light and shadows. Whence it is called *Fosforos* by the Greeks, and *Lucifer*, "bearing light," by the Latins. For it is bright, the moon is brighter, and the sun is most bright. Therefore, understand that star as poetics, which is bright when compared with mechanics, just as Hesper is bright when compared with others. Eloquence is brighter than poetics; philosophy is the brightest. Therefore, in this book understand that bright star to be bright poetry, the brighter moon to be brighter eloquence, the brightest Phoebus to be brightest philosophy. The Hesperian shore, therefore, is the beginning of poetic study.

[6–8] *Semina*, sparks. People say that Virgil here considers natural fire to be within rock. It is indeed a true opinion that certain creatures consist of the four elements, because they are constituted from all four: thus man has choler from fire, blood from air, phlegm from water, and melancholy from earth; likewise, he has heat from fire, breath from air, drink from water, and food from earth. Indeed, certain things are composed of the elements but not from all the elements, rather only from two or three; thus, if rocks had anything of fire, they would naturally be soft; if anything of air, they would inhale and exhale. Thus we find the properties of earth or water in rocks, since we know them to be cold and heavy. Nonetheless, here *semina flammae*, "sparks of flame," are called *abstrusa*, that is, hidden in flint-hard veins (*in venis silicis*), since in the striking of flint sparks seem to come forth, because they are brought forth by air from a collision in which air is trapped between two bodies violently struck together and is thus heated and made glowing by the violence of the collision. *Pars* is to be noted: when Aeneas's companions are occupied—some in seeking fire, some in getting animal lairs, some in searching out rivers —Aeneas hastens to Apollo's temple, because, although some serve the fervor of passion and some search for temporal goods and some prize the humors of feasting and intoxication, the rational spirit withdraws to the study of wisdom alone.[15] Following the poetic fiction, we understand the sparks of flame to be the beginnings and causes of lechery, which are the base thoughts of the lascivious soul. Therefore, they are said to be hidden in veins of flint, that is, secreted away in the innermost thoughts of indiscreet persons. Animal lairs (*tecta ferarum*) are temporal goods in which there are beasts, that is, men transformed by vice into beasts. For the angry are lions, the unclean are swine, and the quarrelsome are dogs. Avaricious men seize these lairs.

[9] *Pius:* since piety is naturally in Aeneas. *Apollo:* historically, Apollo was a wise man who greatly prospered in medicine and discovered a medicinal method (that is, the musical method) and cured the sick with his songs. Circe and Aesculapius are said to have been his children because they were his imitators. And Circe discovered surgery, that is, medicine which uses cauterizing, incision, and other manual operations. Whence it is called *cirurgia*, that is, the work of the hands. Allegorically, however, Apollo is a figure of wisdom. Therefore, he is said to have the Muses as companions, because there are nine Muses who accompany wisdom: Clio, thought leading to learning; Polyhymnia, memory for retention; Terpsichore, delight in studying; Erato, the discovery of likenesses; Melpomene, perseverance in thinking; Thalia, the giver of ability; Calliope, the best voice; Euterpe, proper desire; and Urania, the heavenly Muse, which is understanding.

[9-13] *The Sibyls:* some say there were ten Sibyls; others say three: Herophile, the daughter of Marmensus (who, people say, gave Tarquinius her books concerning the fates of the Romans); Cassandra, the daughter of Priam; Deiphobe, the daughter of Glaucus, to whom Aeneas came, according to the truth of history, as Dares Phrygius writes.[16] Interpret the Sibyl about whom we spoke earlier to be understanding.

Arces: "the citadels" are theology, mathematics, and physics, which in knowledge surpass all the other arts. *Altus:* lofty in comparison with poetics, mechanics, and eloquence. Or, philosophy is called high because through theology one comprehends lofty matters. *Presidet:* "Apollo presides," that is, the wisdom of the theoretical—theology, mathematics, and physics. Thus, wisdom presides because theory is contained in wisdom and because theory is discovered for the sake of wisdom. Indeed, there are four evils which infest human nature:

ignorance, vice, inexperience in speaking, and need. These four evils have four contrasting goods: wisdom opposed to ignorance, virtue opposed to vice, eloquence opposed to inexperience in speaking, and sufficiency opposed to need. For acquiring wisdom one needs instruction in theory; for eloquence, experience in speaking, for virtue, practice, for necessity, mechanics. And thus Apollo presides over theoretical matters. *Horrende:* because understanding discovers divine matters, it more quickly inspires us with awe of them and with an admiration of their arcane nature. Thus the Sibyl is called Deiphobe, that is public awe of philosophy. *Antrum:* "the cave" is the profundity of philosophy. *Secreta:* it is secret because heretofore it is unknown to Aeneas. *Immane:* philosophy is immense because it is inexhaustible. For the more deeply we investigate philosophy, the more fully shall we know our own ignorance. Whence in Boethius philosophy is said to be of "inexhaustible vigor" (*Consolation,* bk. 1, prose 1. 1). *Cui Delius mentem inspirat:* Delius (that is, the bright one, wisdom) instills discretion into this Sibyl through instruction. *Vates aperit futura:* the prophetess (since she is wisdom) discloses the future: according to wisdom, he who sees the present foresees the future. For if one sees the sterility of the earth, he will judge future famine and similar matters. Now Aeneas and some of his companions approach the grove (*iam subeunt*).

[14–34] *Dedalus:* Virgil says that Aeneas approaches the grove of Trivia (*Trivie*), that is, the study of eloquence, and he shows the nature of it. This is done by instruction in the authors. Indeed, the poets introduce one to philosophy, whence Macrobius calls their volumes "nurses' cradles" (*Commentary* 1. 2. 8). Here follows a summary of the story of Daedalus. Those who enter Apollo's temple see the pictures of history and fable on the outside. The temple of Apollo is the philosophic arts; those entering should first understand pictures before writing so that they may pay attention to stories and fables, and this is the reason why in the portico pictorial history and fable are displayed. *Dedalus ut fama est:* according to historians, Daedalus was a certain wise man who prospered in mechanics after he gained experience in the other sciences. We read that he made a cow for Queen Pasiphaë, who, enclosed in it, was violated by a bull. I think that this means nothing more than that he made a chamber in the shape of a cow, in which a young man named Taurus violated her. Then Minos, seeing him, very prudently threw him into chains, that is, he bound him into service. Finding himself in chains (that is, in service), Daedalus travelled the aerial paths with feathers (*pennis*) and came to Apollo's temple—that is, by reason and intellect he contemplated the sublime and inwardly moved himself to philosophical study, and he there dedicated the oarage of his wings (*alarum remigium sacravit*), the exercise of reason and intellect.[17] *Enavit ad gelidas arctos:* Daedalus meditated, inquiring by philosophy why the northern regions are frozen and examining other stars astronomically. *Immania templa:* the arts—instruction, theory, or anything philosophical. *In foribus:* in the approach to the arts, namely, in the authors. *Letum Androgei:* these fables outside the temple represent all the fables of the poets and hence are not to be understood allegorically. *Contra respondet:* Athens is opposite Crete. *Monimenta:* signs. *Labor:* the labyrinthine house, as if interior labor.[18] *Omnia perlegerent:* Aeneas and those who came to the temple with him, that is, those who propose to come to philosophy, read all the playful fables of the authors.

[34-37] *Achates:* one must here note that Achates was omitted from Aeneas's society when Aeneas began to linger with Dido. For as long as Aeneas dwelt with Dido, Achates was not among them. When, however, Aeneas goes to the underworld, Achates is restored as a companion. This clearly shows that as long as Aeneas is detained in lechery, study is abandoned; indeed, when he exerts himself in meditation, he regains study. *Premissus:* after he had come to the Hesperian shores, Aeneas sent Achates through the groves and under the golden roofs to the Sibyl. When she approaches Aeneas, she finds him occupied in looking at the pictures and takes him to the temple. The most useful and fitting order of learning is shown in this, if anyone diligently pays attention to the steps of discipline. First, Aeneas comes from the ocean to the Hesperian shore, that is, from fleshly passion and the excitement of temporal things to the beginning of poetic study; when he devotes himself to that work, then his learned and quick soul can grasp

more difficult matters in all languages (Greek, Latin, or whatever). And immediately he ought to go from the shore to the groves of Trivia, that is, from the beginning of poetic study to the arts of eloquence so that he might learn to speak competently by grammar, dispute by logic, and persuade by rhetoric in the language which he already knew. And then Aeneas ought to send Achates under the golden roofs so that he might bring back the Sibyl, that is, he ought to undertake study of the quadrivium so that he might acquire understanding. For these arts of the mind bring new light to the eye confused by bodily senses. Then he must come to the entrance of the temple and should look at the pictures. After instruction and preparation in the trivium and quadrivium, he who comes to authors easily understands in them grammatical constructions, logical arguments, and rhetorical speeches by applying to the authors the knowledge gained in the quadrivium. *Sacerdos:* she is a "Priestess" because she reveals the principles of both philosophy and eloquence. *Regi:* since the spirit commands and rules the body. *Non hoc:* when Aeneas delights too much and applies himself too long in poetic speeches, understanding rebukes him, telling of other matters. *Tempus:* your age.

[38–39] *Iuvencos septem:* the seven bullocks which move diversely are the seven movements which lead the body in different directions: movement forward, backward, right, left, above, below, circular. They must sacrifice (*mactare*) the bullocks, that is, check attentively and, in a way, kill and resist the body everywhere. We also understand the seven sheep (*bidentes*) to be the seven members of the body, that is, two hands, two feet, torso, head, and genitals. We properly understand the sheep to be the bodies prone on the earth like animals and having no clarity of thought; in contrast, we understand goats climbing high places and looking sharply everywhere to be spirits thinking about lofty matters and discerning them clearly. It is necessary to sacrifice sheep before we come to the temple, that is, to restrain and mortify the members of the body before we approach the arts. *Grege intacto:* from the uncorrupted multitude of thoughts. *Lectos bidentes:* the principal members. In another way, we can interpret the seven bullocks to be those practicing the seven virtues which vex the flesh:

Book 6   41

abstinence, moderation, sobriety, chastity, sparingness, modesty, and shame. Abstinence is one's determination not to anticipate the time of eating. Moderation checks immoderate appetite for food by the rule of reason. Sobriety restrains excessive drinking. Chastity is continence restraining the motion of passion by the moderation of counsel. Sparingness is not exceeding the measure in food. Modesty is moderation in bodily adornment and in the use of furnishings. Shame is the constant repression of disgraceful and unnecessary words. These seven bullocks are plowing the earth, that is, afflicting the body; they are to be sacrificed, (*mactari*) and they come from a pure herd (*de intacto grege*), from the pure multitude of virtues. There are also said to be seven sheep which pertain to simplicity and gentleness; they are innocence, friendship, concord, piety, religion, affection, and gentleness. Innocence is purity of soul, which abhors committing any wrong. Friendship is reciprocated good will towards another equal. Concord spontaneously and communally joins fellow citizens and compatriots in the established laws of society. Piety bestows both a benevolent sense of duty and a conscientious honor upon those joined by blood or citizenship. Religion is a virtue of a certain superior nature which brings forth what is called divine care and worship. Affection is good will held to lesser degree. Gentleness moves the soul above the adversity of oppressors. Understanding urges the offering of these seven sheep.

[40–44] *Affata:* the Sibyl speaks to Aeneas when understanding urges something spiritual, and the men (*viri*) are those who labor manfully. *Teucros:* "the Trojans" are those called to such a complete sacrifice; *sacerdos:* the Sibyl is a priestess because she discloses divine matters; *vocat Teucros in alta templa:* she calls the studious to the high temple, that is, to the philosophic arts. *Excisum:* here Virgil sets forth topography which allegorically describes philosophy when he says that the Sibyl called Aeneas to her. *Latus Euboice rupis excisum in antrum:* "the flank of the Euboean rock carved out into a cave"—a certain part of philosophy is set apart in profundity. The rock (*rupis*) is called philosophy, not the knowledge but the art. The philosophic arts are called rocks, because they are unbreakable. The philosophic arts are of such integrity because none of their principles can be in error. Whence Boethius says, "The robes of philosophy are made from indestructible matter" (*Consolation*, bk. 1, prose 1. 3). These rocks are called Euboean because they are in Euboea, that is, in knowledge. Part of the Euboean rock, that is, part of the philosophical arts, is theory, and the other part is practice. The theoretical part of philosophy is set apart, that is, it is set off by itself. It is divided into theology, mathematics, and physics. Theory concerns itself with those things which practice does not investigate, namely incorporeal matters. And since there are three classes of the incorporeal, there are three types of contemplation itself. The first class of the incorporeal is completely removed from the body, in which class are the Creator, His wisdom, the world soul, and the angels, which are contemplated in theory through its first branch, that is, through theology, which is so called because it is the study of divine matters. The second class is also incorporeal and is that incorporeity which concerns bodies in terms of number and dimension; these are considered in the second branch of theory, mathematics. The third branch of theory also comprehends the incorporeal, namely physics, which considers the nature of things. Theology contemplates invisible substances, mathematics, visible quantities of visible things; physics, the invisible causes of visible things. Thus theory is divided into three branches, and Aeneas goes into the cave, that is, into profundity. Philosophy is called both lofty and deep; it is called lofty in comparison to poetry and other matters, as we said earlier, or because it speculates about divinity; it is deep because it is found to be inexhaustible. The Sibyl's cave is called theory because the Sibyl, that is, understanding, is the grasping of those things whose theoretic aspect is contemplation, and in that theoretic aspect lies a grasping of divine matters, and that is understanding. *Quo:* at the entrance. The entrance to the cave is the disciplines of teaching (which are a hundred—*centum*—in number, that is, innumerable). Every single teaching of the Stoics, Peripatetics, Platonists, Pythagoreans, and all others is an approach to philosophy. *Hostia* is explanation; *centum*, infinite; *unde*, from which sacrifice; *voces*, learning. One should note that in this place there is a double office of wisdom, namely, to give counsel to those who seek it and to educate those who do not. Indeed, Virgil notes by *responsa* the counsels given to petitioners, and by *voces* the learning given to those not seeking it. *Limen:* the will to know. *Virgo:* the Sibyl is a virgin because she joins nothing impure to herself.

[45–47] *Fata:* fate is the temporal outcome of things foreseen. Three Fates have been established, and their names and functions correspond. One of the three goddesses is Clotho (interpreted as evocation), who carries the distaff. We understand her to be generation. Generation is the entry into substance: the beginning of the substance of a thing is called evocation of substance, for she calls forth a thing from nonbeing into being. She carries her distaff because she sustains the beginning of human life, and from this beginning follows the course of all life as if it were a thread from the distaff. The second is Lachesis, whose duty is to pull out this thread, that is, to conduct life from its beginning. She is alteration, the movement from one age into another, from lesser to greater, from greater to lesser. For instance, after a man is born, he progresses from lesser to greater; for the members, paltry at first, grow larger with increasing age. One does not at first have all the powers of the mind: what reason and memory are there in infancy? In adolescence these are regained, and so the movement from lesser to greater continues to manhood. Gradually, from manhood to old age there is a loss both of the strengths of the body and the powers of the mind, and so the movement is from greater to lesser; therefore she is called Lachesis, that is, alteration. The last one is Atropos, whose duty is to cut the thread, that is, to end the sequence of life, which we understand to be corruption, that is, death. Thus, she is called "Atropos" (that is, without turning), since "what is born dies, but the dead are not born."[19] *Poscere fata:* therefore "to ask the Fates" is to inquire philosophically about the origins of generation, alteration, and corruption in things. *Deus ecce:* because Sibyl urges him to ask the Fates, she shows him how. It is not amazing if understanding says, "Behold God" (*ecce Deus*), since understanding is the comprehension of divine matters. *Fanti,* the one who teaches;

ante fores: the entrance. She is said to give a warning before the entrance, because such a warning to understanding compels those at the entrance to go in.

[47–55] *Vultus:* a person is known by his face. The Sibyl's expressions are the infinite effects of understanding, the infinite ideas of infinity. *Color non unus:* beauty, surely infinite, for however much one draws from her, she seems that much more beautiful, and thus according to the capacity of diverse men she has infinite beauty. *Non compte come:* the subtle judgments (as if slender hairs) which lack color. Such is understanding: it does not seek the ornate colors of rhetoric, because it has natural beauty. If anyone should speculate about incorporeity in disciplines where understanding dominates, such as mathematical theorems and theology (sacred writing), he will find almost no adornment of rhetorical colors. For this reason, embellishments are found in rhetoric so that rhetoricians and poets (but not philosophers) may adorn their speeches, because philosophical speeches have their own adornment in their integrity. *Pectus hanelum:* "her breast swells"—the breast of understanding, the breast in which understanding resides, inspired with the fervor and desire of learning. *Rabie:* study is called a frenzy or idleness since it is so considered by inexperienced persons. *Fera:* severe. Wildness is a vice beyond the limits of the virtue of severity, and therefore here it is taken for severity. *Tument:* they overflow. The Sibyl becomes taller (*major*) since she had already spoken in human manner, but she is about to speak in the divine mode, and therefore she appears greater. Just as Boethius, when he describes Lady Philosophy, says she is of changing stature—"For at one time she keeps herself with the stature common to all people, at another time she surges to Heaven" (*Consolation*, bk. 1, prose 1. 1–2)—the same is here understood of the Sibyl. Philosophy or understanding restricts itself to the common measure of all people as long as it demonstrates what is evident to the senses. For understanding, as Boethius says, contains everthing which is inferior to the ideas of the soul, namely, sense, imagination, and reason.[20] The common measure of men is therefore called sense, since it is common to all living beings. Sense, imagination, and reason leap to Heaven when they consider heavenly matters. The

Sybil is human as long as she considers sensual matters or things subject to reason; she is indeed perceived to be greater (that is, divine) when she comprehends matters which humanity does not perceive by sense or even by reason. These are the sure ideas of divine matters and the future outcome of things which made her appear greater when she prepared to reveal them to Aeneas. She predicted future wars which we will explain in their proper place. *Videri nec mortale:* she seemed not human; *sonat:* she told about past or present matters, but in those future things which understanding taught, she sounded not human but divine. Indeed, that divine matter will be explained in order: to know or teach the future is considered divine. And thus foreknowledge of future events is called divination, as if *divina notio,* "divine thought."

Afflata numine: inspired by the power (*numine*) of God; *numen* is so called as if *dei nutus,* "the power of God." Understanding is inspired by divine power—by divine desire—because without that, understanding could not ascend to such things. *Propiore:* to know more is to ascend to God. *Cessas:* understanding urges Aeneas to make offerings (*vota*)—petitions and requests. Likewise, Plato says in the *Timaeus* that divine aid is to be invoked in both the greatest and the least matters.[21] For unless man accepts the divine gifts, he cannot attain knowledge. *Ora attonite domus:* the sacrifices of the arts are various teachings. *Non dehiscent:* they will be ignorant until they make offerings; unless one desires it, he will not have the spirit which teaches inwardly, and unless the spirit is within, he who teaches labors with empty words. *Conticuit:* thus far has the Sibyl advised him. For understanding urges nothing more fully than that we should desire the good and seek with prayer what we desire.

[56] *Phebe:* Aeneas's prayer following the Sibyl's exhortation ought to be read primarily as narration, although it pertains somewhat to the allegory. *Miserate:* Phoebus founded the city with the assistance of Neptune. Laomedon by his own wisdom founded it, and from the confluence of the seas he supplied many necessary things by trade. *Dardana:* one reads in the poets that Apollo killed Achilles by Paris's hand. Dares Phrygius writes that after Hector's death the Greeks and the

Trojans had a long, firm armistice, and that it was permissible for the Trojans to go out to the Greek camp and for the Greeks to go into the city (*The History of the Fall of Troy* 27. 34). It happened that, on a certain day when the Trojans were celebrating Hector's annual funeral rites, Achilles came into the city to see the sacrifice with Antilochus, Nestor's son, and there, having seen Polixena, the king's daughter, and simultaneously having fallen in love with her, he promised that if she were given to him, he would take the army back to Greece or be a future aid against the Greeks. Then Hecuba, a very astute woman, sought a conference with him in Apollo's temple. During this conference, Paris, lurking behind Apollo's statue, shot an arrow to avenge his brother Hector and killed Achilles; therefore it is said that Apollo killed Achilles with Paris's hand. If we take this allegorically, we interpret Phoebus to be the Creator himself, who always pitied the labors of Troy, because He makes the labors of the body pass away, and He nourishes the body with helpful things. He likewise killed Achilles with Paris's hand. Achilles, as if *acherelaos*, means *dura tristitia*, "harsh sadness": for *a* is *sine*, "without," *chere* is *leticia*, "joy," *laos* is *lapis*, "stone." Paris, in the proper interpretation, means sense.[22] Indeed, Paris's arrows are the rays of the two eyes by which Achilles is killed, that is, sadness is extinguished.

[59–63] *Duce:* defender. *Maria obeuntia:* having passed through the excitement of temporal things and the passions of the flesh; *terras:* bodies now given to eartly things. *Massilium gentes:* the multitude of vices. *Arva:* the members of the body. *Syrtibus:* attractive dangers. The Syrtes are the attractions of the water, which we interpret as vices. *Italie fugientis:* unattained growth, for no one in this life can attain the greatest growth. *Hac Troiana tenus fortuna:* the fate of the flesh; note Virgil's splitting of the word *hactenus*. *Genti:* by the powers of soul of those residing in Troy, that is, in the body—namely, wit in the outer suburbs but reason in the center, and so on (we have previously described these dwelling places of the powers of the soul).[23]

[64] *Dii et dee:* virtues and knowledge, or the goddesses Pallas and Juno. One reads that the three goddesses Juno, Pallas, and Venus approached Paris so that he might judge which of

them should have the golden apple. We interpret Pallas as the life of contemplation; Juno, the active life; Venus, the life of pleasure. The golden apple is the greatest good because of both its matter and form: because of its matter, since, as gold, it surpasses all metals, and thus this good exceeds all other; and because of its form, since that form lacks beginning and end, and thus it is the highest good. It is properly called an apple, since fruit is expected from honest labor. But which of these goddesses should have the apple is debatable. For certain people such as philosophers prefer the contemplative life over the others; certain people such as politicians, the active life; certain people such as the Epicureans, the life of ease over the active and the contemplative. Venus seems more beautiful to Paris, because sense places contemplation and action below pleasure, and therefore Pallas and Juno take revenge upon Troy. Because it is pleasing for sense to wallow in pleasures, it is very painful to the flesh to contemplate or act. *Obstitit:* the body resists.

[67] *Regna:* the virtues in which the soul reigns. *Fatis:* outcomes. *Latio:* growth, for Latium and Italy are the same. *Teucros:* the powers of the soul.

[68] *Deos:* in terms of the narrative, Minerva and Cybele, whom Aeneas brought to Italy. Minerva, as if *media vel intima cogitatio,* "central or innermost thought," is wisdom which resides in the brain. For there are three things which furnish perfect wisdom: wit, the power of discovering; reason, the power of discerning what is discovered; memory, the power of retention. In the brain there are three chambers which others call ventricles: in the anterior chamber is the exercise of wit; in the middle, the exercise of reason; in the posterior, the means of memory. Therefore wisdom is called innermost thought. Cybele is so called as if *cubele,* that is, solid earth, which (alone among the four elements) is solid. Thus it is surrounded by the other three elements—by water, air, and fire. Because it is the nature of solidity to be encircled and constricted, and because fire is not at all encircled, therefore fire is thin and fine; air is more dense because it is compressed by fire; water is more dense because it is compressed by both fire and air; and earth is most dense (solid) because it is compressed by fire, air, and

water. Hence Plato in the *Timaeus* (31B) says that there is no solidity without earth. People say that Cybele has a turreted crown because of its stones and sublime construction. She is the mother of Ceres, Bacchus, and Pales. Ceres is the natural power of the earth producing crops; Bacchus, the natural power of the earth producing wine; Pales, the natural power of the earth producing pastures. According to Virgil's narrative, Aeneas brought Minerva and Cybele (that is, the exercise of wisdom and the cultivation of the earth) to Italy.[24] He calls them deities (*deos*) insofar as they pertain to the interior intellect, the interior powers of the soul; he calls them wanderers (*errantes*) because in man's first age they have wandered. *Agitata:* stirred up by excitements of the flesh.

[69–70] *Phebo:* thus far the prayers and now the vows to Phoebus, that is, to wisdom. *Trivie:* eloquence. *Templa:* what memory has preserved. *De marmore:* here Virgil notes the origin of memory. Indeed, wit and memory have diverse origins. For wit arises from a fiery nature, memory from a cold nature. All velocity arises from fire, whence we see that sanguine people are swift but heavy. Wit is speed in seizing the knowable. And so it has its origins in heat. In contrast, memory is the slowness and retention of what is comprehended. For all slowness arises from cold. Whence we see melancholic people are slow but thin. Martianus allegorically notes these diverse origins when he says that Urania resides in *Aplanes* (the firmament), that is, by seizing strength in fire; Polyhymnia resides in Saturn, that is, great memory resides in coldness.[25] Virgil notes the same things here when he says *templa de marmore*, "marble temples," that is, the preservation of memory by tenacious cold.

[71–73] *Te quoque:* O you, understanding. *Penetralia:* deep reservoirs. *Nostris regnis:* as long as we shall rule by controlling vices. *Hic:* in these reservoirs of memory. *Sortes:* prophecies. *Archana fata:* secret, divine dispositions. *Dicta:* revealed by you. But how they were revealed will be evident in what follows. *Genti:* partnership; everything which she tells Aeneas's spirit about things to come she will also tell to his companions, that is, those living spiritually.

[73–74] *Electos:* those pure of vice. *Alma:* "the soul," since it is of divine substance and understands the divine. *Viros:* one must note that men, not boys or youths or old men, are devoted to understanding. In the first ages there is an excess of heat; in old age, however, an excess of cold and humor. Temperance is in manhood, and therefore the first ages because of excessive softness and the last age because of excessive harshness do not understand, but moderated manhood does. Whence Plato says that human life is comparable to a wax tablet which, if it is excessively hard or soft, will take no impression, but if tempered retains the figure.[26]

[74–76] *Foliis:* unstable and wandering teachers who are fickle and straggling about. *Carmina:* your precepts. *Ventis:* by the vices of instability. The Sibyl entrusts her verses to leaves, because by means of unstable teachers intelligence educates us in her own precepts. *Ipsa:* she indeed sings while she instructs us by her inspiration. *Canas . . . finem:* you, Sibyl, inspire understanding, because the spirit demands this alone.

[77–82] *At Phebi:* She begins to show how she conducts herself, and then understanding predicts future events. *Vates:* "the prophetess" of Phoebus, since she discloses philosophical matters. *Nondum paciens:* not yet at rest; for the more she knows, the more she expounds. *Immanis:* since she touches heavenly matters. *In antro:* in the depths of the mind. *Baccatur:* she labors or studies. Studying is almost like raging, whence also we have defined study as the vigorous application of the mind with the greatest desire to do something. *Si possit excussisse pectore:* "so that she might discharge the god from her breast," as doctrine is sent forth from the mind. *Magnum deum:* Phoebus, namely, wisdom. Understanding sees that wisdom enriches others by teaching, and therefore, understanding bequeaths wisdom to them; and since understanding sees that wisdom is angry with the greedy possessor by whom she is held, then understanding flees, and therefore Solomon warns, "My son, let your springs be drawn off."[27] *Fatigat:* the Sibyl swells up, since he who intoxicates is himself intoxicated. *Os rabidum fera corda domans:* that is, restraining the excesses of the mouth and heart. *Fingit premendo:* wisdom forms and teaches by holding back from illicit things. *Hostia domus centum:* the limitless nature of philosophical teaching. *Ferunt:* they offer. *Auris:* by temporal processes.

[83–86] *O tandem:* understanding shows how much may be allowed to the spirit after one has come to the increase of virtue and wisdom. *Pelagi:* the sea of the world or the flesh. Or we interpret the sea to be temporal life, since the violence of the winds stirs it up. We interpret the winds to be the twin temporal fortunes, prosperity and adversity, which come quickly and, moving across, pass quickly, and they diversely seize ships, and they lead the minds of men navigating that sea into the shipwreck of vice. Whence Boethius calls them earthly winds *(Consolation,* bk. 1, meter 2. 4). We again take the sea as temporal life with this simile: a storm at sea begins in the deeps and extends itself to the heights. For the earth's moisture (that is, natural vapor) first stirs up the bottom, and this commotion excites the seals sleeping on the bottom. When the seals come to the surface of the water, sailors are frightened, knowing that the tempest has already begun at the bottom. So too in temporal life, passion and misery spread themselves from its beginning to its end. *Terra:* in the solidity of virtue. *Graviora:* although there are many dangers for the soul in fleshly desires, in the solidity of virtue there is such arduousness and difficulty that they can scarcely endure. *Lavini:* the reign of labors. *Dardanide:* the powers of the soul. *Curam:* fear. *Non volent:* "they shall wish otherwise," for when the soul in the difficulties and struggles of virtue and in the midst of the infestations of vice returns to the pleasures of pure desires, the soul generally grieves because of its honest purpose. *Bella:* since the future events which she foretells are narrated in the remaining books, we therefore put off an interpretation of them for the present. It will be sufficient here to have known this much—that understanding predicts the future wars of vice to the spirit hastening toward virtue and wisdom, so that it may face them more bravely when they come: "For whatever we foresee wounds more lightly."[28] Again, she foretells these future misfortunes not so that he may come to them in the slack security of negligence but so that he may gird himself to endure them.[29]

[98–101] *Talibus:* thus far the prophecy of understanding. *Ex adyto:* out of the secret of the mind; *horrendas:* since the foreknown infestations of vice frighten the spirit; *ambages:* "enigmas," since she promises both adversity and prosperity, or *ambages,* as if ambiguities, that is, complex interpretations of the allegory. *Antro . . . remugit:* she speaks again in his mind so that he may remember. *Obscuris:* poetic fictions; *Vera:* for with poetic fictions she conceals the truth. Intelligence especially teaches divine things; therefore, the poetic fictions especially correspond to divine matters, because, as Macrobius says (*Commentary* 1. 2. 18), the divine is to be concealed by the veil of words. Thus Plato and other philosophers, when they speak about the soul and about other theological matters, avail themselves of poetic fictions, just as Virgil does in this work.

[101–5] *Frena:* recollection. *Stimulos:* incitements. Wisdom urges souls to investigate divinity and attracts them to its secrets. *Furenti:* since understanding transcends human capability in discerning the present and in foretelling the future, the Sibyl is said to rave. For it is a human habit that whatever one does not see in himself he considers impossible, but what he does see in himself he considers possible. Thus Sallust: "What anyone finds in himself he accepts with a calm spirit; but if something exceeds that, then he takes true ideas as false" (*The Catiline War* 3. 2). *Furor:* prophecy. *Animo:* by discretion.

[106] *Unum:* the rational spirit seeks nothing except to know the Creator through knowledge of creatures. *Ianua:* the doors through which we enter the underworld, the region of the fallen—the terrestrial habitation in which we are born. *Regis:* we said that this king is the earth and is called Dis, since all riches are found on earth—money, treasure, estate, ornate goods. Whence Boethius:

In the deepest caves the earth nourishes whatever pleases and excites minds here. [*Consolation,* bk. 3, meter 10. 13–14]

[107] *Thenebrosa palus:* the Lethean lake—forgetfulness clouds the mind. We said previously that Lethe is forgetfulness, Styx is hatred, Phlegethon is the ardor of the wrathful, and Acheron is sorrow. These four rivers in the lower regions refresh the infernal inhabitants because in this region mortals are animated when they draw from these four rivers. All the forgetful drink from Lethe; the malicious, from Styx; the irate, from Phlegethon; the sorrowful, from Acheron.

[108] *Ire:* we have taught before in the fifth book why the

descent to the underworld must be made: so that Anchises (although he is elevated over all things) may be seen, because knowledge of creatures leads to contemplation of the Creator. *Conspectum:* contemplation. *Ora:* presence, but in this life one attains contemplation, and then in the other life one attains vision—that is, he sees face to face.[30]

[109] *Doceas:* "you will teach"—for that is the nature of intelligence. *Iter:* the ascent through the knowledge of creatures. The first step is from the inanimate to the insensible animate, as, for example, from rocks to plants and trees; the second step is from these to the sensible but irrational animate, that is, from trees to brute animals; the third step is from the irrational to rational animals, that is to men; the fourth step is from the human to the celestial. Understanding sees that man, even though he has an immortal soul, nonetheless must be freed from the nature of a body, and therefore understanding ascends to celestial matters seeking greater things, and in these it discovers angels to be greater than man, because they are immortal, incorporeal, and free of all carnal contagion. The fifth step is from the angels to the Creator. Since understanding judges angels to be higher than other creatures, so it requires something still higher than the angels, because it sees that angels have an origin. And therefore it has gone through the order of creatures to the Creator. *Hostia:* the doors are knowledge about creatures. *Pandas:* you will open. Here is an example of *histeron proteron*, a reversal of logical steps. For first is "to open the door," and then is "to ascend on the journey." But, following the steps noted above, Aeneas cannot ascend without the Sibyl as a guide.

[110–17] *Illum:* Aeneas persuades by his personal deeds. *Flammas:* the fires of passion. *Tela:* the infestations of vice. *Humeris:* with thoughts. *Hoste:* he who wishes to take himself from vice. *Comitatus:* by protecting. *Maria:* passions. *Pelagi:* the commotions of temporal things. *Minas:* infestations. *Celi:* the winds of air, that is, the vices. Or, *minas pelagi:* the infestations of the flesh; *minas celi:* the errors of the soul. *Ferebat:* "he endures" with forgiveness. *Invalidus:* one is weak in those matters in which there is more vice than virtue. *Ultra:* "beyond" the virtues or merits of age (*senecte*), for Anchises is eternal.

Orans: exhorting piously. *Mandata:* commanded knowledge; for whenever Anchises admonishes and whenever Aeneas delays as if unwilling, then Anchises "regally adds threats to his pleas."[31] *Patris:* by leading me to what he desires. *Potes:* having recognized his obligation, Aeneas in his prayer shows the possibility of fulfilling it. *Omnia:* for the Sibyl knows the human and the divine.

[118] *Hecate* is the goddess having a hundred powers; people say she is the moon which has infinite effects. Here we interpret her to be divine wisdom, which is called Hecate, that is, a hundred powers since she contains in herself ideas of infinite things. Hecate controls understanding in the lower world, since wisdom subsumes understanding in temporal matters because wisdom knows them perfectly, and wisdom by knowing the divine transcends understanding. By the testimony of Boethius, understanding grasps all those inferior powers of the soul (*Consolation,* bk. 5, prose 4. 26–36). There are four powers of the soul, and the superior know all the inferior, but the reverse does not hold.

Virgil calls temporal goods groves (*lucos*) since they have three qualities similar to those of a grove. Just as groves are dark because of the lack of sun, so too temporal goods are dark because of the lack of reason. And just as woods are impassable places because of the multitude and variety of paths, so too are temporal goods impassable because of the various paths which seem to lead to the highest good but which do not. And *Avernus* means "woods without spring" (*nemus sine vere*), as if without delight; and thus the groves lack true delight.

[119–20] *Si potuit:* Aeneas persuades the Sibyl by example. *Orpheum:* we read that he was the son of Apollo and Calliope, and he had a harp which drew out trees and rocks, stopped rivers, and calmed beasts. He was the husband of Eurydice; when she was wandering in the meadows, the shepherd Aristaeus fell in love with her. While fleeing from him, she stepped on a serpent, was bitten, and died from the poison. Moved by grief over this, Orpheus descended to the underworld so that he might bring back his wife, charmed the lords of the shades, and regained his wife on the condition that he would not look back. He looked back and lost her. We interpret Orpheus to be wisdom and eloquence. Whence he is called Orpheus, as if *orea phone*, that is, *bona vox*, "good voice." He is said to be the son of Apollo and Calliope, that is, of wisdom and eloquence, for the wise and eloquent person is the son of wisdom and eloquence. She is called Calliope, that is, *optima vox*, "the best voice," because eloquence makes the voice fluent. Orpheus has a harp, that is, rhetorical speech in which diverse colors as if diverse strings resound. With his soothing remedy he urges sluggards to honest work, calls the unstable to constancy, calms the truculent; and therefore it is said that he draws out rocks, stops rivers, and calms beasts. Eurydice is his wife, that is, he is naturally joined to natural appetite. For no one is without natural concupiscence. Whence one reads in poems that there is a certain genius, a god of human nature, which is born and dies with a man, as Horace says: "a god of mortal human nature in each head" (*Epistles* 2. 2. 188–189). We understand that to be the natural appetite which dominates human nature, and it is called Eurydice, that is, the appetite for the good, for it is given in order to seek the good. She wanders about through the meadow, that is, she errs through earthly things which in a way flourish and immediately dry up, because all the glory of the world is like a flower of the field.[32] While Eurydice wanders, ambling here and there, Aristaeus falls in love with her. Aristaeus is interpreted as divine virtue: *ares*, that is, *virtus*, "virtue," whence *Ariopagus*, that is, *villa virtutis*, "the house of virtue"; *theos* indeed means *deus*, "god." This virtue is called divine because man has something divine in himself. The function of a shepherd is given to him since it is the duty of virtue to watch over the flock, that is, the multitude of thoughts, words, and deeds. Aristaeus wishes to join Eurydice to himself: virtue wishes to join appetite to itself so that appetite may seek only good and abhor evil. Fleeing Aristaeus, Eurydice treads on a serpent in the fields (in this earthly life she encounters temporal good). The serpent is called temporal good because it crawls through lower things, and, although it appears beautiful, it is deadly. The serpent's bite poisons her: the delight of temporal good infects sense. Having received the cause of death (delight in temporal good), she is drawn to the underworld (she is led away to temporal things and abandons heavenly matters). Moved by desire for his wife, Orpheus goes to the underworld: he descends by thought to temporal matters so that, once he has seen their fragile nature, he may withdraw his appetite from them. He charms the lords of the shades, that is, the possessors of temporal good. After he has sung for a while (after he has there exercised wisdom and eloquence), he regains his wife (he removes appetite from earthly matters) with the stipulation that he will lose her if he looks back (if he thinks again about the temporal). Virgil here notes this descent of Orpheus. *Manes coniugis:* dead appetite, which dies when it is separated from the true life, the heavenly good. *Thracia:* since he first thrived there. *Fretus cithara:* armed with rhetorical speech; *fidibus:* with adorned rhetoric.

[121] *Si fratrem:* one reads that Castor and Pollux were brothers; Pollux was a god, and Castor was a mortal. Since indeed Castor could not as a mortal live forever, it is said that Pollux shared his divinity with him and descended to the underworld so that Castor might ascend to the heavens. Some people interpret them as two stars, one of which has divinity because of its greater brilliance, and the other has mortality because of its lesser brilliance. And when Pollux descends to the lower hemisphere, Castor holds the higher, and thus Pollux descends to the underworld so that Castor may rise. And people say that *alternam mortem* is "the other setting": for when one sets, the other appears, and conversely. But, in a better way, we interpret these brothers to be the soul and the body, of which the soul is rational and immortal and thus a god, but the body is mortal. The soul endures the death of the body for a time, so that the body may then share the immortality of the spirit. For just as the soul dwells in this region of death by companionship with the body, so too the body dwells in the region of life by companionship with the soul. *Alterna morte:* with changed mortality. The body gives the soul temporal mortality so that the soul may give the body eternal immortality.

[122–23] *Thesea:* Theseus is called divine and good, for *theos* is *deus,* "god," and *eu* is *bonus,* "good." We interpret Theseus as the rational and virtuous man. He descends to the underworld according to the descent of virtue. *Alcides* is interpreted as the strong and beautiful person by whose strength and deeds we understand that the glory of deeds is beautiful. Whence he is called Hercules, as if *gloria litis*, "glory of dispute": *her* is *lis*, "dispute"; *cleos* is *gloria*, "glory." He also descends following the same descent of virtue, as will be discussed later.

[124–31] *Aras:* the virtues of the soul upon which duties and incense (prayers and good works) are sacrificed to God. *Sanguine:* in the species. *Facilis:* "easy" because it openly shows human nature. To descend to the underworld is easy, but it is difficult to return. For anyone can descend to the temporal through knowledge and habit, but hardly anyone can return. When men are full of illicit things and human nature is greatly weakened and yielding to vice, it is easily kept there. But although those who descend are infinite, nonetheless there are three kinds who return: those whom Jupiter loves, those whom virtue raises up high, and those who are demigods. Since Jupiter is *iuris pater*, "father of law," (or, Jupiter, as if *iuvans pater*, "the helping father"; or, Jove, as if *yavis*, that is, *universalis vis*, "universal strength"), he is the highest god. It is said that he especially loves those persons whom he has drawn unconquered from temporal things, such as Paul.[33] *Noctes:* ignorance. *Dies:* knowledge. *Gradum:* desire. *Auras:* serenity; the lower winds are temporal goods, the superior are eternal. *Labor:* difficulty. *Opus:* usefulness. To return is laborious and useful; to remain is easy and useless. *Ardens:* fiery, tending upward like fire. Vice, on the other hand, is earthly; that is, it looks downward. Thus virtue is fiery because it gives the fervor of love of God and because it leads to the heights and because it makes the man of the higher dwelling place powerful and patient. Whence no man will be able to dwell there if he does not have virtue first, as Lucan says:

There dwell the semidivine spirits, which fiery virtue made innocent because they endure in the life of the lower heavens. [*Pharsalia* 9. 7–9]

Dis geniti: the children of Apollo are wise; the children of Calliope, eloquent; the children of Jove, rational. They are demigods, that is, they are rational and immortal in soul but mortal in body.

[132-35] *Silve:* temporal goods, as was said earlier. *Cochitus* means lamentation. Thus this river surrounds the underworld, because no one descends to the underworld without lamentation. Whoever comes to the underworld according to natural descent crosses this river. When a man is born, he begins to cry (which is indeed appropriate) since, coming from the warm and moist womb to the cold and dry earth, he suffers. Therefore, a warm and moist bath is immediately prepared for him. Likewise, whoever descends by the descent of virtue crosses the river Cocytus: seeing such frailty in temporal things, he weeps when he sees men so devoted to that frailty. Likewise, whoever descends by vice or by the rites of sorcerers also crosses the river Cocytus, because he, either repenting his delights or suffering punishment, cries. And since, as it were, there are four gates by which one comes to the underworld—that is, nature, virtue, vice, and artifice—he who enters through any gate crosses the river Cocytus, and so Cocytus flows in a curve (*sinu*), in a riverbed which is passion or sorrow. *Bis:* Aeneas descends "twice," since everyone descends once through nature. *Indulgere:* to satisfy.

[136-37] *Latet:* before anyone can go to the underworld, the Sibyl warns him to seek the golden bough; if this is neglected, there is no path at all open to the underworld. This bough is found on a shaded tree (*arbore opaca*), and we shall show how this is to be interpreted. Allegorically, anything which is composed of diverse parts (such as the virtues, the vices, and knowledge) is called a branch. Therefore, the golden bough (*ramus aureus*) is here interpreted as philosophy, since just as a branch has smaller branches, so too philosophy is like a tree with two branches, namely the theoretic and practical, which in turn are subdivided as the following figure shows.[34] It is golden (*aureus*) because we interpret gold to be wisdom, whence one reads that four virgins—Aglaia, Hespera, Arethusa, and Medusa—watched over the golden apple; by this we understand that study, wit, reason, and memory bestow wisdom.[35] Understanding advises Aeneas to seek this branch so that the path to the underworld may be accessible, since knowledge of things is not open to one lacking in philosophy. This golden bough is on a tree (*arbore*). Pythagoras called humanity a tree which is

divided into two branches, that is, into virtue and into vice. For although they are joined together in the beginning, some people divide themselves to the left and some to the right, some in vice and some in virtue. This tree is shaded by the heaviness of the flesh. Since humanity is divided like a tree, so here it is called a "tree," and it is depicted by Pythagoras as the letter *Y*, forked like a tree. *Latet:* in the depths of the mind. *Foliis:* with the colors of words. *Vimine:* opinions.

[138] *Iunoni:* the goddess of Erebus is Proserpina, whom Pluto carried off, and he takes her back to the upper world for half the month, and he does not permit her to leave him for the other half; she is the daughter of Jupiter and Ceres—of fire and moisture. Ceres is so called as if *creans res*, "creating things"; Proserpina is the moon, and she is so called as if *iuxta serpens*, "near the serpent," since it is nearer the earth than the other spheres. Pluto (the earth) seizes her (the moon), since the earth by giving heaviness to the moon keeps it away from the ethereal region. Ceres searches for her with torches because in the heat of flames moisture is needed to prevent scorching. For half the month Proserpina is sent to the upper world, and for the other half she is united with her husband, because the moon for half the month is seen in the upper hemisphere, and for half it is in the lower region of the earth. She is the Queen of Erebus; her husband is the king, since the coldness of the earth and moisture of the moon are dominant in the fallen region, and the region of mutation lies between the earth and the moon. The altar of this goddess is the posterior cell of memory in which, as noted earlier, are coldness and slowness, which come from the moon and which serve memory. And therefore it is said that the branch is sacred to this goddess since in that cell philosophy is entrusted to memory. *Inferne Iunoni:* to the infernal queen; the proper name *Juno* is shared.

[139–40] *Lucus . . . tegit:* the collection of temporal goods hides the bough, because temporal goods so impede that the beauty of philosophy cannot shine forth. *Umbre:* images of good. *Telluris:* of earthly good. *Operta:* manifest nature. *Subire:* through knowledge.

[142–48] *Discerpserit . . . sibi:* he will have received instruction at her altar. *Pulcra:* clear. *Primo:* the Sibyl says this lest Aeneas object that "the branch has been taken long ago." *Avulso:* received by instruction, for the teacher's wisdom does not diminish for the sake of the student's wisdom. *Virga:* the mind of a student is trained like a branch in different directions. Therefore (*ergo*), since one must have the bough of philosophy, he must find out by reason and intellect what is to be done, and, having discovered it, he must do it. *Manu:* by work. *Volens:* for wisdom says, "I love those who cherish me" (Prov. 8:17). *Fata:* divine dispositions. *Viribus:* by studies. *Ferro:* with the sharpness of wit. *Duro:* natural.

[149–55] *Preterea:* understanding urges him to seek the golden bough, but it first urges him to bury Misenus. Misenus, the trumpeter of Aeolus, competed with Triton and was killed by the god. He must first be buried before the descent to the underworld is possible. Misenus is so called as if *miso enos*, that is, *laus caduca*, "fallen praise," because *miso* is *obruo*, "bury," and *enos* is *laus*, "praise," which we interpret as temporal glory. He is from the region of Aeolia because "love of praise vainly swells with a windy voice."[36] He carries a trumpet, that is, the windiness of pride which, as long as he plays (that is, as long as he praises someone), incites battles. We said that Triton, the god of the sea, is annoyance of the flesh, which likewise plays the trumpet, that is, by lamentation. Misenus competes with Triton, but it is ambiguous which one incited the battle more: whether it was the proclamation of praise, which is Misenus's usual story, or whether it was the voice of lamentation demanding vengeance, which is Triton's trumpet. Nevertheless, Triton killed Misenus, since annoyance of the flesh destroys appetite for glory. Burying Misenus is committing glory to oblivion (which understanding advises). *Ante:* Aeneas must bury Misenus before he descends because, according to Fulgentius, "he who does not bury the pomp of empty praise will never penetrate the secrets of nature."[37] And therefore the Sibyl says *preterea*, "moreover": beyond what is necessary to search for the bough another labor remains. *Corpus amici:* the magnitude of the glory which you have loved thus far. *Exanimum iacet:* mortal and fallen, because Misenus does not reach heavenly matters but is prostrate. *Heu:* "alas," since you followed what you did not know (*nescis*) to be fallen. *Incestat:* he defiles. *Sedibus:* to oblivion. *Pecudes:* vices.

[156–77] *Mesto:* since no one of such perfection is found who, cheerfully, puts aside glory. *Lumina:* reason and intellect so that Aeneas may discover the bough; *vultu:* by desire. *Linquens antrum:* that is, leaving flesh. *Cecos:* making man blind again. *Eventus:* prosperity and adversity. *Volutat:* he searches. For at first when the mind begins to philosophize concerning temporal good by distinguishing between bad and good fortune, it looks toward the highest good as if by a certain comparison of opposites. Boethus observes this sequence.[38] *Animo:* by discretion. *Fidus:* since study does not abandon him unless he abandons it. *Vestigia figit:* he assiduously pursues consideration of the visible and invisible. *Vario:* by first considering one matter and then another. For this is the custom of debaters. *Humandum:* forgetting. *Litore:* the withdrawal of passion; *sicco:* from the abundance of passion. *Hectoris:* since he had attained glory because of integrity. *Lituo:* by praise. *Hasta:* by pride. *Equora:* the commotion of temporal things. *Concha:* with the mouth of adulation. *Divos:* powers of the soul. *Certamina:* for he says that he sings better, that is, that he advises better than reason or anything else. *Saxa:* sharp and harsh labors. *Unda:* the inundation of adversity. *Ergo:* because he prepared an altar (*aram*), that is, a mound of virtues. *Sepulcri:* of oblivion.

[178–89] *Arboribus:* we have called trees anything divided into species. Interpret these trees here to be the virtues divided into kinds, just as we have in rhetoric.[39] It would not be easy for me to introduce their definitions here. *Celo educere:* to raise all the way to celestial substances. For this mound of virtues is to be increased until man touches the celestial through it. *Itur in antiquam silvam:* since it is impossible to build up that mound of virtues unless the eradication of vices comes first, because "unless it is a pure vessel, whatever you pour in turns sour" (Horace *Epistles* 1. 2. 54). Therefore, Virgil first shows how vices are eradicated and then how virtues are implanted. *Itur in silvam:* Aeneas "enters the woods"—he advances with the steps of contemplation (namely by wit and study) in the multitude of temporal goods, which are shady and trackless.

Antiquam: born from the beginning of time. *Stabula:* dwellings filthy with the stench of vice. *Alta:* falling into pride. *Ferarum:* men transformed by vice into bestial nature. For philosophy calls lecherous men swine, fraudulent men foxes, babbling men dogs, truculent men lions, wrathful men boars, rapacious men wolves, and sluggish men asses.[40] All of these dwell in temporal goods, just as in contrast "the conversation of the good is in Heaven" (Phil. 3:20). *Procumbunt:* they are uprooted. *Picee:* because of their bitterness and sterility, interpret these four trees as vices. Since we noted before that trees signify whatever is divided in philosophy, we then understand virtues or knowledge by sweet and fruitful trees, but vices or ignorance by bitter ones. Pine trees are prickly on top but smooth below and thus figure the passions, at first delightful but then pungent with the pains of repentence and conscience. For when passion recedes, "it will greatly sting hearts with fierce vexation" (Boethius *Consolation,* bk. 3, meter 7. 5–6). Boethius calls these vices sterile thorns *(Consolation,* bk. 1, prose 1. 9). *Sonat . . . ilex:* the ilex is a tree covered with a tough and impenetrable bark, which we interpret as obstinancy of soul which bursts out in words of defense when instruction corrects and rebukes it. Virgil properly says *icta securibus,* "stricken with axes"—rebuked by other instruction. *Securibus:* with reprimands. *Sonat:* the tree resounds with the clamor of rebuke. *Fracxinee:* this lofty ash tree figures forth pride. *Robur:* having shown the eradication of vice, Virgil indicates the implanting of virtues. The easily split oak (*robur fissile*) shows any vice capable of being broken down. For there are vices which, when they are broken down, are returned to virtue: just as in the case of avarice (which is "to possess what should be possessed and what should not be possessed"), we should separate it from ourselves and cast off what is useless and thus possess what is useful; in the case of prodigality things are pursued "to give what ought to be given and what ought not to be given." And thus by cutting away and casting off the useless and adopting the useful, the contrary vices are broken down to one mode (that is, to "give what is to be given and to possess what should be possessed"), and that is munificence. It happens in the same way with the vices of cowardice and rashness and the other contradictory vices. Whence Virgil says, "It is cleft with wedges" (*scinditur cuneis*), that is, by judgments of discretion. *Ornos:* those acorn-bearing trees figure the fruitful virtues. which Aeneas's men draw (*advolvunt*) to themselves laboriously. *A montibus:* from divine substances. For the mountains are sometimes interpreted as the vices of pride, as in "the mountains melted like wax" (Ps. 96:5; Mich. 1:4), and sometimes as the rational and divine substances, as in "the mountains around Jerusalem" (Ps. 124:2) and "the mountain is raised above all mountains" (Is. 2:2). *Inter talia:* eradication of vices and implanting of virtues. *Socios:* philosophers. *Armis:* the arms by which the enemy is attacked and friends are defended are three powers of the soul, namely, irascibility, concupiscence, and boldness. *Accingitur:* the soul is fortified. For when both good and evil here and there surround Aeneas, he offers irascibility to the bad, concupiscence to the good, and boldness to both, for with boldness he seeks the good and attacks the bad. *Tristi:* eagerly and anxiously. *Aspectans:* contemplating by reason. *Precatur:* his prayers are his desires. *Si:* "if only!" *Heu:* Aeneas bemoans Misenus's death, since he had been his companion; that is, he mourns the weakness of fallen glory because the soul had pursued it.

[190–203] *Fatus erat:* he had desired. *Columbe:* reason and virtue. Reason is the natural knowledge of things to be done, and virtue is the voluntary exercise of that knowledge. *Sub ora:* they come into his sight since they precede his contemplation. *Celo venere:* from the Creator, through the angels, to man. *Sedere:* to choose a place; *viridi . . . solo:* in living bodies. *Maximus:* divine. *Maternas:* in the narrative the doves are called the birds of Venus because they are lecherous: whence they are called *columbe,* "doves," as if *colentes lumbos,* "dwelling in the loins." Aeneas's mother (as was said previously) is harmony. Therefore they are maternal, that is, harmonious, because reason without virtue is idle, and virtue without reason is ignorant. *Auras,* temporal goods, because of their instability. *Lucos:* the multitude of things. *Dives ramus humum pinguem opacat:* wisdom overshadows humanity rich with virtues—for indeed wisdom is of such splendor that it shows human nature to be weak when compared with wisdom. *Dubiis:* since the end is not known; *re-*

bus: contemplation. *Diva:* concord. *Effatus vestigia pressit observans . . . signa:* the soul, wishing for all of this, restrains the senses and diligently notes everything instructive or admonishing. *Pergant:* they perservere. *Pascentes:* growing. For instruction is enriched by its practice. *Volando:* surveying the heights. *Acie:* with sharpness of vision. *Oculi:* study and wit. *Sequentium:* of rational and virtuous souls. *Fauces:* the earthly entry of Avernus (*Averni*), of the sublunary regions; *olentis:* stinking, offensive to reason. For a stench is discovered there, and the stench of the region is fallen and corruptible nature. *Tollunt:* the doves rise up. *Lapse:* reason and virtue turn back to earthly things from heavenly things, so that they may know these by comparing them. *Gemina:* "twin," because humanity is divided as if into two branches, which Pythagoras shows by the letter Y. Or *gemina,* because of the two sexes, or because humanity is composed of corporeal and incorporeal substances.

[204–11] *Unde:* from which tree. *Aura:* temporal good. *Discolor:* for wisdom is immortal, but temporal good is mortal. The one is incorruptible, the other corruptible. The one is true, the other false. *Per ramos auri refulsit:* these contraries are disclosed by the concepts of philosophy.

[205–9] *Viscum:* as if Virgil had said "*gummi,*" "gum," for just as that liquid gum goes from the interior to the exterior of the tree, so wisdom, flashing from the mind of man, also comes to the exterior either through instruction or action.[41] *Brumali frigore:* "in the cold of winter," which solidifies the sap coming from the interior of the tree; thus the coldness of old age by restraining vice serves wisdom. *Fronde:* so wisdom flourishes in its work, and this work exfoliates from man like a leaf from a tree. For the leaves of this tree are works, and the fruits are rewards. *Quod non seminat:* the tree does not produce the gum. For just as the exterior moisture moves from the earth by means of roots and the innermost pith, so too wisdom from a teacher flashes through the mind or speech or deed of a pupil. *Croceo fetu:* that is, with the beautiful effect of wisdom. *Circumdare:* wisdom protectively surrounds bodies having a round form—that is, human heads, because in them are the five senses and the other beginnings of wisdom, namely, the instruments of wit, reason, and memory. *Frondentis:* fructifying.

Bractea: interpret the golden leaf as philosophical knowledge; interpret the soft breeze as rhetorical speech, which is called a breeze. For wind is air in motion: every voice is air moved through natural instruments. It is soft because it soothes its listeners' souls. *Leni vento:* in persuasive speech gold leaf (*bractea*) rustles (*crepitat*), that is, philosophical thought is spoken (as has been explained). *Avidus refringit:* fervent with love of wisdom, he takes on the labor of study. *Sub tecta:* in the mind.

[212–25] *In litore:* in the beginning of philosophizing. Like Diogenes, they wept (*flebant*), because they had been pursuing such a fallen thing. *Cineri:* the remains. *Principio:* he shows what is uppermost (*suprema*). *Piram:* the heap of virtue. *Ingentem:* surpassing all the things of fortune. *Pinguem tedis:* overflowing with the fires of virtue, and *robore:* with virtue. *Secto:* we have talked before about this splitting; a split oak is to give what should be given and to possess what should be possessed, another is to dare what should be dared, fear what ought to be feared, and so on in other matters. And these logs indeed are those which have been set aside from what was cut. *Latera:* the four principal virtues. *Frondibus:* with sombre (*atris*) works which bury passion. *Cupressos:* cypress and figs are trees which, when planted in graves, penetrate the rocky matter and appear on the outside. These trees figure knowledge which, when placed within through instruction, is brought to the outside by speech. Persius notes this figure when he says, "What has the fig tree shown if not that passion and what is born within will burst forth?" (*Satires* 1. 24–25). *Ferales:* away from divine ideas. *Constituunt:* they build together. *Armis:* as was discussed before, "shining" (*fulgentibus*), since virtues are set in practice. *Latices:* water naturally flows downward, quenches thirst, and cleanses dirt in washing. So too instruction moves from the superior to the inferior (from teachers to students), it refreshes those who thirst with the fervor of wisdom, and it also cleanses vice from the flesh; thus it flows downward, refreshes, and cleanses. *Aena:* vessels of water—those freed by wisdom. There are many examples of water being interpreted as wisdom. For it is said, "You will give them the water of wisdom," and "God weighs waters in a measure," and "He places the seas into treasure houses," and "the heavens which are above the waters," and "Secret waters are more sweet."[42] *Flammis:* that is, with thought, because just as flame heats cold things, so thought enlivens listless members. And likewise, just as ferns and bushes in the field are burned off by flames, so too in the soul noxious desires and vices are eradicated by thought. *Corpus frigentis:* the extent of numbness. *Ungunt:* they anoint the body. *Fit gemitus:* lamentation, as discussed before. *Membra reponunt thoro:* they store up glory into the soul. *Purpureas vestes velamina:* the beautiful and transitory applause of the people. *Pars:* the weak ones who know what is fallen but nevertheless follow it. *Subiere:* they carry him on a bier *(feretro)*—that is, in their souls as if in funerary urns, vessels of fallen glory. *Triste:* "they are sad" because conscience saddens those who follow what they know to be fallen. *Facem:* the ardor of virtue and the splendor of knowledge. *Aversi:* hostile to that glory. *Tenuere:* to exercise. *Cremantur:* destroyed. *Turea:* "incense"—adulation and praise which in a way give off an odor. *Dapes:* fame.

[225–35] *Crateres:* in the poetic fiction we interpret this as bodies; thus in Macrobius you have the constellation of the Bowl of Father Liber (Bacchus) placed between Cancer and Leo *(Commentary* 1. 12. 8). From this the descending spirit drinks, and drunkenness follows. Interpret in this manner: when the sun is in Cancer, because of its nearness its more vigorous rays attract excessive water, so indeed a certain star placed there is called *Sirius,* as if *attractans,* "attracting." Thus, this aquatic sign has the name of an aquatic animal. And therefore this sign figures moisture; the lion, heat. And the region between Cancer and Leo is air, between the heat of fire and the moisture of water. In this region is the Bowl of Father Liber, that is, the human body, first in terms of powers, since the heat and moisture of this region create and enliven it, and second in terms of location, for even if the body is said to be of the earth, we know it to be above the earth. It is called the Bowl, because it is the vessel of the humors. The drink is the heaviness of the flesh which the soul incorporates, perceives, and accepts while it descends, and this is what it drinks. From this drink follows drunkenness—oppression and weakness of the natural powers. Such bowls are scorched with torches, that is, they are made fine by virtue. Misenus was accustomed to drink from such bowls. The drinks by which Misenus is refreshed are brightness of form, speed, health of members, and other things which are in this vessel. *Olivo:* the instruction and exhortation by which the flame of virtue is kindled. Those freed by this flame have lamentation in the bowl (that is, the body), which we interpret to be the working of reason in the mind. *Cineres:* the corruptible residue, namely the final praises. *Reliquias:* fantasies—vain imaginings. *Vino:* teaching. *Favillam . . . bibulam:* interpret thus: as ashes soak up water, so fantasies destroy instruction. *Coryneus: Coron* means *pulcrum*, "beautiful," hence *Coronides* is *pulchra forma*, "beautiful form," and *Corinna* is *pulchra mulier*, "beautiful woman"; *neos* indeed means *novum*, "new." Coryneus therefore means *pulcritudo novitatis*, "beauty of newness," the delight of new knowledge.[43] *Ossa . . . texit . . . aeno . . . cado . . . socios . . . circumtulit:* new knowledge buries glory in endless oblivion and strengthens those engaged in philosophy. *Ter:* "three," as pertains to the soul. *Unda:* instruction. *Pura . . . rore . . . levi:* purging by the water of learning and diminishing the heaviness of vice. *Ramo olive:* with the virtue of peace. *Domos:* minds.[44] *Novissima:* the perfection of doctrine, by which glory is held in contempt and hatred. *Mole:* the mound of virtues. *Remum:* human labor. *Tubam:* the wind of praise. *Monte:* divinity. *Misenus:* the mountain is called Misenus since he hated glory.[45]

[237] *Spelunca:* here one must note the simple course of magical descent. According to the narrative Aeneas uses magic (as noted before). But how he did so is shown here as well as the excellent place and the quality of the sacrifices; in addition, the appropriate time for this is also shown.[46]

[268–72] *Ibant:* Virgil returns to the philosophic descent. *Obscuri:* Aeneas is seen by no one except himself and the Sibyl, and the Sibyl by no one but herself and Aeneas, because only understanding knows the spirit, and only the spirit knows understanding. *Nocte:* in temporal life. For day is eternal life. *Umbram:* natural ignorance. *Domos Ditis:* the halls of Dis are temporal goods, because earthly nature prevails in them. *Vacuas et inania:* the halls are empty because they are useless. *Iter in silvis:* contemplation about temporal goods. *Iupiter condidit celum umbra:* the body, which is comparable to Jove (air), darkens divinity by natural ignorance. *Per incertam lunam:* at night, that is, through uncertain (namely temporal) life. *Sub luce maligna:* with distorted knowledge of human nature. *Nox:* this life. *Rebus:* invisible things. *Colorem:* beauty. For this life interferes to prevent everything divine from appearing beautiful to us. [273–81] *Vestibulum:* the surface of earth. *Faucibus:* birth. *Cure:* anxieties. *Malesuada:* that is, wickedly persuading: for hunger urges the five excitements of gluttony—to advance meal time, to seek more sumptuous food, to devote oneself to painstaking preparation, to desire with excessive appetite the foods which are seen, and to exceed the measure in eating. *Consanguineus:* for just as death does away with the motions and senses of the body, so sleep does the same for a time. *Gaudia:* pleasures. *Limine:* birth. *Bellum:* "the war" between the body and the spirit. *Eumenidum:* the Eumenides are the three daughters of Night and Acheron, namely Alecto, Tisiphone, and Megaera. We interpret Acheron as sorrow (as we said before) which begets three sisters on Night, that is, on the ignorance of the spirit. The first is Alecto, who is interpreted as distorted thought; the second is Tisiphone, voice applied to wicked thought, and that is wicked speech; the third is Megaera, wicked deed.[47] *Talami ferrei:* stubborn hearts; *crinem:* the multitude of quarrels. *Vittis:* arms of war.

[282–84] *In medio:* all of these things are in the entrance, that is, on the surface of the earth. Beyond this is the house of dreams, the elm (*ulmus*) laden with branches and leaves, having a single dream under each leaf.[48] A dream is the resting of the animal powers, the repose of the five senses. Its house is the human body, and an elm tree properly figures it. For just as the elm does not bear fruit but nevertheless sustains fruitful vines, so too the flesh is spiritually sterile but nevertheless is the fruitful home of virtues and knowledge. The elm is full of branches and has a great growth of limbs; it is leafy, as if laden with false leaves, that is, vain thoughts, under each of which deceptive ideas are conceived. Philosophy discusses how a dream may occur in the human body, for it teaches that there is a certain inward fire in our bodies. The fire is kindled out of all the elements, but since this fire has heat and light, its light (as Plato says, *Timaeus* 45B–E) works through the eyes giving vision. Its heat digests food and soothes the members with vital relaxation. Now, after digestion (since, as was said above, digestion involves four humors—liquid, steam, foam, and sediment) the steam ascends by the nature of lightness and fills the important chambers of the senses; and thus, sight being blocked at the gates (that is, at the pupils of the eyes), the fire rushes through the limbs to the relaxed body; and, the humors being dissolved and passing through the cleared passages, repose strengthens the body. *Annosa:* growth over a certain space of years. *Opaca:* natural ignorance. *Vana:* dreams coming from others kinds of thoughts are false.

[285–86] *Ferarum:* vicious people. *Centauri:* we read in fables that Ixion desired to sleep with Juno and that she interposed a cloud which, receiving Ixion's seed, gave birth to the Centaurs, who were part men and part animals. We therefore interpret Ixion as the sun, which is called Ixion, that is, *super omnia*, "above everything," since the sun, placed above everything, illuminates everything. *Iuno*, as if *iuvans novos*, "helping the new," is called the earth, since it nourishes the recently born with its fruits. Ixion wishes to lie with Juno when the sun sends both its heat and dryness below. Juno interposes clouds when the earth produces mist against the approaching heat. After the heat of the sun mixes with this moisture, temporal goods are produced and are therefore called Centaurs, because they are partly rational and partly vicious, that is, because they are human in the forepart and bestial in the hindpart; and thus we understand the Centaurs as biformed of horse and man because they first see the rational and then run quickly. *Stabulant:* they have a stable, a house filled with the steam and stench of vicious men.

In fables, Scylla is called a monster, having canine groins below a virginal face. This monster figures dissimulators who offer blandishments and (as it were) a virginal appearance but have canine barking within, that is, malicious detraction.

[287–88] *Centumgeminus:* the hundred-handed Briareus, begotten from the forms of a hundred animals, as from a lion, boar, dog, swine, wolf, and infinite others. He signifies the worthlessness of someone created from infinite vices because he has the lion's savagery, the dog's ceaseless yapping, the boar's rage, the wolf's deception, the swine's filth, and so on.

Belua: the Hydra is a multiheaded, serpentine monster. Whenever one head is cut off, more grow in its place. People say that literally and historically this monster was the many arms of the sea: whenever any one of these might be blocked up, infinite rivulets spread out from it. But we interpret the Hydra allegorically to be ignorance containing many ambiguities, which the infinite heads signify. Winding signifies nothing else than what diverts the ignorant person from one thing to another. We interpret Hercules as wisdom, and his name is appropriate: in Greek he is called Hercules, which in Latin means *gloria litis,* "the glory of dispute"—for *Her* is *lis,* "dispute," and *cleos* is *gloria,* "glory." Hercules cuts off one of the Hydra's heads when he determines one ambiguity of a problem, and then others grow in its place. Indeed, Hercules, seeing his useless labors, burns up the Hydra: a wise man, seeing his study insufficiently useful, burns up ignorance with the most vigorous fire of the mind when he investigates ignorance with the fervor of inquiry and illuminates it with the splendor of knowledge. Boethius notes that intellect is expressed with this poetic fiction when he says that a question ought to be burned "with the most vigorous fire of the mind" (*Consolation,* bk. 4, prose 6. 3). *Lerne:* of corporeal nature. *Stridens:* sounding frightful (*horrendum*) to the ignorant.

Chimera is a triform monster; the forepart is a lion, the midpart a goat, and the hindpart a serpent. Historically, people say the Chimaera is nothing but a mountain having lions at the peak, sheep on the slopes, and snakes at the base. But philosophers interpret the Chimaera as passion offering the rage of a lion at the beginning (in sight, in encouragement), having the goatish and stinking practice of copulation in the middle, and the stings of serpents in the end (the pangs of penance and bad conscience). *Flammis:* with ardor.

[289] *Gorgones:* we read that the Gorgons—Sthenno, Euryale, and Medusa—were the three daughters of Phorcys, the god of the sea; but they are called by the common name "Gorgons." These three are said to have had only one common eye, which they shared among themselves. We read that Perseus killed the

third one with the help of Pallas and Mercury. The horse Pegasus was born from the drop of blood which Medusa shed. A spring gushed forth when Pegasus touched the ground. Phorcys is the god of the sea, the spirit which rules in the flesh (as we interpret the sea), and he is called Phorcys, as if *formans rerum conceptiones,* "forming the ideas of things"—for *orche* in Greek is *conceptio,* "idea," in Latin. He begets three daughters: the first is bad desire (called Sthenno)—weakness, because the first weakness is to wish evil; the second is concealing the good (Euryale), which is wicked speech because it conceals the good by detraction; the third is wicked practice (in Greek, Medusa)—terror, for we fear her more than the others. *Gorgon* is the name common to them, as if *georgon,* that is, *terram colens,* "cultivating the earth," since they attend the flesh. The single, common eye which Sthenno gives to Euryale and Euryale to Medusa is bad conscience, which Statius calls "the fierce day of the spirit" (*Thebaid* 1. 52). This bad conscience is first had in wicked desire, then in wicked speech, and finally in wicked deed. Perseus is interpreted as virtue. With the help of his sister Pallas and his brother Mercury (wisdom and eloquence), he kills the third wicked sister (wicked act), and he does this by the written law which is the sword edge of Mercury. Note that he did not kill the other two sisters but only the third, for virtue is unable to restrain evil desire or evil speech by any law. A drop of blood then fell (after wicked deed had been killed), and the bloodshed stopped (the savage men having been called from the bestial way of bloodshed). The winged horse Pegasus signifies fame because fame is "swifter in growth and more changeable than any other evil" (*Aeneid* 4. 174–175); its speed is properly signified by an animal of twofold swiftness. It has speed born in the feet of a horse and in the wings of a bird. This Pegasus is born from a falling drop of blood, that is, in the stopping of an outpouring of blood, and he seizes and carries off Perseus to other places: the name of virtue spreads throughout all nations. Pegasus touches the earth when fame excites the human mind. Thus a spring flows forth when wisdom with the stimulus of glory trickles down in instruction.

[289] *Arpie:* the three Harpies are maidens who are covered

with feathers of birds, have sharp claws, and feel hunger in their bellies; the first is Aello, the second Ochiroe, the third Celaeno. They defiled Phineus's table and snatched his food after he had blinded his sons and had then received the same punishment from the gods. But Hercules, received by Phineus, together with Zetes and Calais, the sons of Boreas, killed those birds with arrows. Phineus signifies the greedy person; his name is appropriate: Phineus, as if *epineos*, that is, *supra novitatem*, "above newness," for *epi* is *supra*, "above," and *neos* is *novitas*, "newness." He is so called because he conceals newly acquired things. He puts out his sons' eyes when he returns to his former habits which he acquired through instruction lacking discretion or intellect. He receives the same punishment because he had also lost those same eyes through a sordid use of life. Whence Ovid: "Why, Phineus, do you stab out the eyes of your undeserving offspring? That punishment must redound upon your head" (*Art of Love* 1. 339–40). *Arpia* in Greek is *rapacitas*, "greed," in Latin: for *Arpo* is *rapio*, "seizure," in Latin. Number and name agree that there are three harpies. For it is certain greed to attack someone, whence one of them is called *Aello*, as if *allonedon*, that is, *aliena invasio*, "attacking others." The second is to snatch quickly, and she is called *Ochiroe*, that is, *properata rapina*, "hurried robbery." The third is to hide what is stolen, whence she is called *Celeno*, which is *nigra*, "black," that is, concealing. They are called virgins because they are sterile and bear no fruit. They are birds because they are quick to attack others. The claws are usury and interest, which are the instruments of seizure; the feathers are the instruments of concealment such as purses and satchels; the hungry belly is the ravenous greed for money. They contaminate Phineus's table when they befoul his way of life by urging filth. Whence Juvenal says, "In the middle of September the greedy person holds back mince."[49] They seize his food because they think it is necessary to ruin the victim. For a greedy man "searches, and the wretch abstains from what is found and fears to use it."[50] Phineus welcomes Hercules when a greedy man receives a wise man. Hercules kills the Harpies with arrows when the wise man argues against greed with sharp rebukes. *Zetus* is so called in Greek as if *zelus*, that is, *emulatio*, "emulation," in Latin; *Calais*, as if *calon*, that is, *bonum*, "the good." For emulation here is understood as poetry, which consists entirely of imitation. Whence Plato in the *Timaeus* (19D) says that poets practiced in imitation can recreate the experiences which anyone has from his birth. Read attentively Horace, Juvenal, Statius, and Virgil; they imitate each other in all things. Calais is honest work; Boreas, the wind, is glory, as Horace says: "Whom Glory has borne to the stage in the windy car" (*Epistles* 2. 1. 77). A misfortune: "Glory is nothing but a great wind in the ears."[51] Boreas is the father of Zetes and Calais since glory is the cause of poetry and of great works. For many place the fruit of virtue in glory. Indeed, poets greatly seek glory, to which that verse of Horace testifies: "Whom glory has borne to the stage, etc. . . ." Zetes and Calais help kill the Harpies—poets and satirists and the examples of good work take away the capacity of avarice.

[289] *Tricorporis:* we read that Geryon was a triform monster, whom the historians understand to be a king having three kingdoms. But allegorically Geryon signifies the man of vice who is urged on by three types of vice: latent, manifest, and habitual. His name is fitting: *Gerion*, as if *gerinos*, that is, *terre frons*, "the brow of the earth." And properly he is called "the brow of the earth" since he is carried to such prominence of heaviness. *Forma umbre tricorporis:* the kinds of vice, divided into latent, manifest, and habitual.

[290–94] *Ferrum:* the sword with which Aeneas defends himself from enemies is reason, which resists vice. *Corripit:* he holds a sword in his hand when he exercises reason in work. For he had it in a scabbard as long as he concealed reason in the earthly mind. *Trepidus:* he was afraid that those shadows would rush upon him, that vice would attack him. *Aciem:* offering the sword to fleeting shadows is casting the sharpness of reason before attacking vices. *Vitas tenues sine corpore:* the pleasures which are considered life by the Epicureans—without fruit, without substance. For vices are not of any substance, nor are they natural properties of any substance. Or, *sine corpore:* without strength. The body which is solid properly signifies strength and health. Vice is without strength because it can injure no one unless he first yokes himself to it by consent. Whence vice is comparable to a tied-up dog: just as the tied-up dog can harm no one unless he voluntarily comes to it, so too vice can harm no one unless he voluntarily consents to it. *Volitare:* to encircle human nature, whence one reads that "the wicked walk in circles" (Ps. 11:9). *Cava imagine forme:* "the hollow semblance of form"—the empty similitude of reason or nature which is called form, since substance is known through it. *Irruat:* Aeneas attacks what he ought not to attack, for vices are not to be followed but fled from. *Frustra auras:* it is sufficient to flee from empty and transitory pleasures.[52]

[295–97] *Hinc via:* Aeneas goes from the vestibule (in which are all the previously mentioned forms) to the river Acheron. *Acheron* means, as we said before, "without joy." After leaving behind the above-mentioned forms, Aeneas is brought to Acheron, because when we separate ourselves from vices pointed out by understanding (which is a guide), we are afflicted with intense sorrow. *Hinc:* from these forms is the way (*via*), the passage to Acheron, that is, the sadness coming from abandoned vices, because the habit of them was pleasant, but the rejection of them is mournful. *Turbidus:* the river is murky, since sorrow disturbs the light of reason. *Ceno . . . voragine gurges estuat:* because of the filth of the flesh and the oppression of knowledge, the abundance of sorrow creates surges when it stirs up and enflames the mind. *Arenam eructat:* the sand from which Acheron comes forth is the multitude of injuries and adversities from which sorrow takes its beginning. Acheron casts up this sand when sadness manifests outwardly through great complaint the injuries which it suffered. We frequently see this in tragedies. Acheron cast up sand when the sorrow of Boethius narrated the tyranny of Theodoric, saying, "We are condemned to death and proscription as a reward for true virtue."[53] *Cochito:* mourning.

[298–301] *Portitor:* Aeneas must pass through the aforementioned waters with Charon as guide because it is useful in the process of maturation to pass through grief and sorrow resulting from the abandoned pleasures of vice. We read that Charon, the son of Polydaemon, is a ferryman. He is called *Caron*, as if *cronon*, that is, *tempus*, "time." He is the son of Polydaemon, that is, of the firmament, and he originates from the turning of the firmament. Or he is called Polydaemon, that is, *civitas demonum*, "the city of devils," because that is the region of spirits.[54] Charon leads Aeneas and the Sibyl across the river, because time places us beyond sadness and mourning; in this life, time makes all evil transitory. *Horrendus:* the bristling of hair is the coldness of winter days. Sadness and mourning are called waters (*aquas*), because the minds of miserable men sink down as did Boethius's mind.[55] Sadness and mourning are called rivers (*flumina;* as if *profluvii,* "flowing") because they grow larger by a certain amount. *Servat:* these rivers are under Charon's command since mourning and sadness occur in time. *Scalore:* deformity. *Mento:* Note that every person is described by his greater qualities, and this is also true here. Charon's greater qualities are the winter months. Spring is lesser, as if prior to other things: summer and fall are medial, and winter is ultimate, even though philosophers may disagree about this. The Hebrews say that it was a summer day which dawned before all others. They argue that the earth was separated from the waters in that season for the purpose of being freed from them and of generating various types of animals from the mud; a great amount of heat was necessary, and no vernal but only summer heat was sufficient. Others say that the springtime came first. They say that the tenderness of newly created things could scarcely withstand the fierceness of summer heat; moreover, because all animate things, whether sensate or not, are created, nourished, and grow by heat and moisture, and because spring is temperate in heat and moisture, a spring day was therefore necessary for the first creation. Since the winter months are Charon's most prominent quality, interpret his beard as December, in which there is a great amount of greyness, snow, and hail; and thus the sign of Sagittarius is assigned to them. *Inculta:* sterile; or, *inculta,* as if impeding the cultivation of the earth. *Lumina stant flamma:* the sun and moon possess the fiery region. *Amictus:* the types of storms such as snow, hail, and rain. *Humeris:* winter months. *Nodo:* by the constriction of the cold.

[302–4] *Ratem:* Charon has a stitched and leaky boat, which we interpret as the human body. It is stitched together—composed of diverse elements and humors. It has leaks, the openings of the senses. Charon pushes it with a pole (*subigit conto*); time sustains and rules the body with the nourishment of food. Because time freezes the earth in winter, opens it in spring, dries it in summer, and gives harvest in winter, therefore Charon is said to control that boat with a pole. And properly the pole, namely the sustainer of the boat, signifies the nourishment of the body—its sustenance. *Velis:* the sails which drive the ship by catching breezes are the two eyes which draw the body to different ends through delight of pleasures and the lechery of revellers. As you read in the *Timaeus*, this sense, when something new and therefore delightful seizes it, causes the body to be moved with hasty and inordinate force.[56] *Ministrat:* Charon tends the sails, when time gives light and darkness to the eyes—light by day in order to see, darkness by night in order to rest and be restored. *Ferruginea . . . corpora:* filthy, bodily vices. *Senior:* because Charon originated with matter. *Cruda:* consuming—the antiquity of time consumes much (whence in another poetic fiction you read that Saturn devoured almost all of his children). *Viridis:* because time is renewed in a single year.

[305–8] *Ad ripas:* to the end of vice and the beginning of mourning, sadness, and the other emotions. *Matres:* the crowd (*turba*) which rushed in. In all poetic fictions we interpret mothers and fathers as teachers, sons and daughters as those formed by their teaching—that is, the students. *Vita:* philosophy understands two lives, two deaths, and two graves in poetic fictions. According to the Stoics, one life is the freedom of the spirit dwelling in virtue and knowledge, which the same Stoics call philosophy. According to the Epicureans, the other life is slavery to bodily pleasures, which these persons consider the only life. Thus, the first is life of the soul, the second is indeed life of the flesh. The first death is the end of the first life, the oppression of vice which is true death. The other death is the mortification of vice, which Plato says must be sought by philosophers.[57] He urges this death who said, "Mortify your bodily members" (Col. 3:5). The first burial is the engraving of thoughts in firm memory, in which virtue and knowledge are to be buried. The other grave is the one in which Misenus and Palinurus are to be buried: the enwrapping in oblivion. *Innupte:* the sterile. *Rogis:* with the ardor of vice. *Ante ora parentum:* before the sight of teachers.

[310–12] *Folia:* leaves blown about by wind are compared to minds wandering in the commotion of vice. *Frigore:* the death which comes upon temporal wealth. *Aves:* human minds are compared to birds, since minds with the wings of virtue and knowledge can ascend to the heights. *Ubi, etc.:* just as the coldness of autumn sends birds across the waters, so the oppression of vice forces the minds of men to wander. *Apricis:* the pleasantness beyond the deep is the quiet life of the cleansed beyond sadness and mourning.

[313–20] *Stabant orantes . . . cursum:* they linger in temporal sadness desiring to go beyond (*transmittere*) temporal life, to go beyond the river Acheron into the quiet life of the cleansed. *Manus tendebant:* they undertake works. *Ripe ulterioris:* in the beginning of the quiet life. *Tristis accipit:* harsh time carries them across the river. *Ast alios:* Charon bears some beyond temporal sadness to the quiet life, and he keeps others for a long time (*longe*) from entering into temporal sadness. *Harena:* the bank of Acheron. *Miratus:* it is astonishing when we say that no meritorious person leads the way: since some are born to the condition of always being burdened with adversities, some are free of adversities for a long time, some are carried across the sadness of temporal life to the quiet life. And therefore the spirit consults understanding saying, *"Dic, etc."* *Discrimine:* by degree of merit. *Remis vada vertunt:* by counsel souls traverse sadness.

[322–24] *Certissima:* since knowledge and virtue are the signs of divinity. *Dii cuius:* in the Gigantomachia, when the gods had the help of Victory, the daughter of Styx, and thereby prevailed in battle; from that time they therefore had such reverence for Styx that they feared to swear her name falsely. They are called *gigantes*, "giants," as if *gegantes*, "engendered from the earth"; their bodies are created naturally from the earth and nourished by its food. When people say that Titan is the Giants' father, what else do they mean but that the Giants are engendered by heat acting on the earth? We say that the gods are knowledge and virtue. The Giants therefore declare war on the gods when bodies oppress knowledge and virtue. The Giants are defeated when bodies are mortified. We have said that the river Styx is interpreted as hatred. Styx joined with Mars and begot Victory because victory comes from hatred and battle. Victory is said to favor the gods when virtues successfully dominate bodies. The gods revere Styx because there is no hint of discord between virtue and knowledge. *Turba:* the multitude of sinful people.

[325-29] *Inobs:* lacking good. *Inhumata:* they are not buried because their vices are not wrapped in oblivion. *Quos vehit unda:* those who pass through temporal sadness come to the pleasantness of the quiet life of the cleansed. *Sepulti:* they are enwrapped—their vices in oblivion, their virtues in memory. *Ossa quierunt sedibus:* virtues were placed in the treasury of memory. Bones properly signify virtues, and the flesh signifies vice because; just as flesh is worn away by decay but the bones remain, so vices are corruptible but the virtues cannot be corrupted. *Centum:* a finite period of time stands for the infinite. *Errant:* "they wander," living in vice. *Volitant:* they wander. *Littora:* the quitting of the life of pleasure and the beginning of the life of labor. And note well that they are able "to hover about." For to hover about is to fly imperfectly; they fly, however, but not perfectly, since they come to the bank with few feathers and they cannot cross it; they come with too little virtue and knowledge to quit the life of pleasure and begin the life of labor; and because they are not buried (that is, since they have not put virtue in memory and vice in oblivion), they scarcely cross over. *Stagna exoptata revisunt:* "they look again at the pools they long for"—they again contemplate Acheron and Cocytus, which they desire to pass, so that, having recognized the nature of these agitations of the mind, they may change them.

[331-34] *Constitit:* Aeneas delays by contemplating these things. *Vestigia pressit:* he represses the senses; otherwise, passage across the waters is not open to him. *Multa:* Aeneas considers how certain persons come to temporal sadness and mourning, but others do not. Fortune spares many in comparison with the others, whom she drives to intolerable calamity. Some of these again come to sadness, some cross over to the quiet life, and some not. Aeneas considers these and similar matters. *Iniquam:* people consider such an outcome unjust because some flourish and some are kept back, even though some are reputed to be good, some de-

praved. *Leucaspim:* Leucaspis and Orontes, the two companions who perished in the storms, signify natural knowledge and natural virtue. The human mind has these two by nature, from which it takes their triple seedbeds, because natural knowledge has three seedbeds: wit, the natural power of discovering; reason, the power of discerning what is discovered; memory, the power of preserving what is discovered. Virtue also has three beginnings: irascibility (fleeing evil), concupiscence (desiring good), and boldness in opposing evil and defending the good. Therefore we understand natural virtue by Leucaspis. *Leucaspis* means the enclosure of whiteness or beauty: *leuce* is interpreted as "beauty" or "whiteness"—whence also Leucothoe, as if "the white goddess." *Caspos* in Greek means *claustrum,* "enclosure," in Latin. Thus the sea has the name *Caspian* because it encompasses the eastern regions. The enclosure of beauty is called virtue because it protects the beauty of the soul against the contamination of vice. Orontes, as if *orentheos,* that is, *bonitatis deus,* "the god of goodness," is called wisdom since it is good and divine and since it gives the good and preserves it. Whence in Boethius wisdom is called the "teacher of virtue" (*Consolation,* bk. 1, prose 3. 3). Orontes is called *Licie classis ductor,* "the captain of the Lycian fleet," because wisdom is the advance guard of bodily pleasure—wisdom ought to lead the way in all pleasure. *Cernit:* with the eyes of contemplation; *ibi:* to Acheron and Cocytus. In this life knowledge and virtue are exceedingly oppressed by mourning and sadness, whence Boethius: "Harsh punishment deserved by the wicked oppresses the innocent" (*Consolation,* bk. 1 meter 5. 29–30). *Mestos:* stern persons. *Mortis honore:* burial. We have called the grave the memory of virtue and knowledge, the forgetting of vice. And note that these two men lack the honor of death (*honore mortis carere*), that is, proper burial, since we commit virtue and knowledge to memory with greater difficulty than we do the filth of vice—in wicked things we are mutable. *Vectos equora ventosa:* distracted because of the temporal commotions which were full of wind—the commotions of vice. *Auster:* we have shown earlier that the winds signify the attack of vice. We take this wind to be the maw of gluttony. For this wind bears many clouds: moving from the antarctic pole it comes upon clouds elevated by the heat of the neighboring torrid zone, which it pushes before it into the arctic region. The north wind, however, is calm: therefore, the south wind figures forth gluttony. Just as the south wind pushes more clouds than others, so this vice displays greater ignorance than others. Whence there is a saying of the Greeks: "From a heavy belly comes no refined sense." And Horace attests that this vice "casts down a particle of divine breath to the earth" (*Satires* 2. 2. 79). The Epicureans have erred more than others in doctrine since they have labored greatly in this vice. *Auster aqua obruit involvens naves:* therefore the south wind stirs up waters around Aeneas's companions when gluttony of the first age oppresses natural knowledge and virtue by rushing in and by confusing their desires.

[337] *Ecce:* note that after Aeneas descends to the underworld, his dead companions and all his experiences pass again before his eyes: as long as the rational spirit is inclined to contemplate fallen things, the mortified vices of the first ages return through imaginary representations (as in "Behold, the shade of Palinurus brought itself") whenever the imagination reflects on past errors; thus the shades of both Dido and Deiphobus appear when the remembrance of past pleasure and terror occurs.

[338–40] *Libico cursu:* in the movement from pleasure to the beginning of philosophy. *Dum sidus:* Palinurus scanned the stars—when he, in whom there is error, gazes at heavenly matters—and so Palinurus died. *Exciderat puppi:* this error dropped away from its desire. *Effusus in undis:* slain and overcome by instruction. *Vix cognovit:* because Palinurus had been separated from Aeneas for some time, Aeneas did not know him, and therefore Aeneas is said not to have recognized him, just as the wise and chaste person is said not to recognize passion even though he knows what it is. *Mestum:* error saddens those whom it causes to wander into vice. *Umbra:* retreating.

[341–46] *Prior:* Aeneas speaks first because the wise man properly speaks first. *Deorum:* virtues and knowledge. *Apollo:* wisdom. *Fallax:* Apollo "fails" Aeneas when the wise man by his teaching draws the injurious spirit from error. The wise man does this when he first instructs a person: so in Horace you read that his father taught by examples what should be shunned and what pursued and did not give the reasons but said, "It is better for a wise man to give the reasons why things should be shunned or pursued" *(Satires* 1. 4. 105–6). *Responso:* by his counsel. *Incolumem:* strong. *Ponto:* with the commotion of secular goods. *Fines Ausonios:* the beginnings of growth. *Cortina:* innermost counsel.

[348–54] *Nec me deus:* Aeneas twice asked "which of the gods snatched" *(Quis deus eripuit)* Palinurus away and plunged *(mersit)* him into the sea. Palinurus does not deny that one of the gods cast him off, since that is true, nor does he deny that the god plunged him into the water, that is, that knowledge or virtue had located error in secular life. *Gubernaculum:* the assent of the soul to vice. *Multa vi:* by a certain violence of vice consent is wrung from the will. *Herebam:* error and wicked consent are inseparable. *Precipitans traxi mecum:* for at the same time he dies. *Pro me:* Palinurus knows that vice finds itself a place in many persons. *Quam tua:* Palinurus appears to grieve especially about this because he is separated from wisdom. *Armis:* in thinking, delighting, consenting. *Defficeret undis:* he should have resisted the wicked undertaking with the replenishment of instruction. *Navis:* will. *Surgentibus:* with rebukes.

[355–57] *Nothus:* passion, as we have said. *Noctes tres:* Palinurus's triple ignorance—of himself, of other creatures, of the Creator. *Vexit:* error and ignorance predominate in lechery, so lecherous people think that the disgraceful use of their vice is honest. *Aqua . . . lumine:* he is driven by the south wind for three days in the lake of lechery, and he sees Italy on the fourth *(quarto)*—since the error of passion dwells in three pleasures and, in the fourth, pleasure comes to know growth. Light signifies pleasure, because according to the Epicureans only pleasure is delightful and shining and repays its cheerful follower. The first pleasure is thinking about illicit things, the second is approving of them, the third is doing them, the fourth is persisting in them.

[358–59] In all these things pleasure errs, but in the fourth, error greatly increases itself, and therefore Palinurus is subdued; *paulatim adnabam, etc.:* but note that Virgil says that "scarcely" *(vix)* did Palinurus see Ausonia, because although error rapidly moves toward growth, nevertheless, it scarcely sees itself flourish; all vice blinds its followers so that by their ignorance it may seize greater and greater powers in them. *Adnabam:* "I slowly *(paulatim)* came" through the lake of lechery—by yielding to the heaviness of earth (*terre*) and the strength of necessity and habit, he is brought to the necessity which binds the mind with an indissoluble chain and gives strength to vice; therefore, necessity is figured by the heavy and firm earth. *Tuta:* At this point, Palinurus does not fear he will perish; but because wise men thoroughly overtake error and then discover its habit and then denounce it so that the mind is made steadfast, therefore the fierce tribe (*gens crudelis*) attacks Palinurus—the multitude of stern people.

[360–65] *Gravatum:* confirmed. *Madida veste:* filthy practice. *Uncis manibus:* disposed to evil works. *Prensantem capita hespera:* scaling difficult heights—laborious virtues. *Montis:* of rational substance; *ferro:* with a rebuke; *predam:* which they ought to seize; *ignara:* lacking experience of the true world. *Nunc:* he does not come to the mountain but is repulsed by the force of the wind. *Habet fluctus:* the lake of lechery. *Versant:* the winds (*venti*)—the attacks of vice—bear him away. *Littora:* the approach to the lake of lechery. *Quod:* Palinurus binds Aeneas to an oath—as long as error is in him, he asks the rational spirit to release him. *Lumen:* the eternal good; *auras:* temporal goods; *terram:* firm and fruitful virtue.

[366–72] *Portus:* the beginning of salvation for the libidinous. *Velinos:* since they veil the mind or are born of volition. *Require:* look for those things left behind—seek through contemplation so that you may see me (error). From the beginning we ought to examine error so that we may uproot it. *Divum:* knowledge and virtue. *Dextram:* the just work. *Undas:* temporal events. *Sedibus:* of memory. *Morte:* in mortification of vice. *Quiescam:* virtue and knowledge arise. *Fatus:* vice speaks to the spirit when the spirit learns something about it, or when a person in whom vice exists speaks to a wise person. These matters are easily noted in earlier statements.

[374–83] *Vates:* understanding speaks when the intelligent person speaks. *Inhumatus:* "unburied," unless you wrap virtue in oblivion. *Amnem:* Cocytus. *Aspicies:* in contemplation. *Iniussus:* not predestined. *Fata:* temporal events. *Deum:* of divine ideas. *Finitimi:* those who accede to error. *Prodigiis:* signs. *Ossa:* misleading facts. *Tumulum:* oblivion. *Solemnia:* holy works. *Locus:* the mind which you, Palinurus, dominated is said to wander. *Gaudet:*

vices are said to rejoice because they persevere in corrupting the soul as if that were their joy, since joyous observances appear in them. *Terre:* of the torpid soul.

[384–91] *Iter:* the journey is contemplation. *Navita:* Charon is said to be in Acheron, since a man of greater age sustains greater calamity, as Juvenal proves with King Peleus, who sees "the beard of Antilochus burnt in the flames." Then he adds about old age: "Every kind of disease encircles like a line of troops . . . that one with a weak arm . . . this one, a weak hip; that weak man lost both his eyes and envies the one-eyed"; "With pale lips they accept food from strange fingers."[58] And Horace: "Many discomforts surround old age" and

The approaching years bring many comforts with them and the receding years take many away. [*Art of Poetry* 169, 175–6]

Pedem: the course of contemplation. *Prior alloquitur:* Charon speaks to Aeneas when an old man full of days and much time speaks to the rational person, and he speaks first (*prior*) because old age is prudent and mindful of many things. Therefore because of revered seriousness, the first speech is given to him. *Increpat:* Charon rebukes Aeneas—when a prudent old man sees someone's rational spirit traveling the path of contemplation, he fears lest he may be descending merely because of curiosity or for the love of temporal goods alone, and therefore the Sibyl responds that Aeneas has come to see his father, that is, to know the Creator. *Armatus:* an unsheathed sword, as we said before. *Quid:* why have you come—for love of temporal good or contemplation of temporal good? *Comprime:* stop; *gressum:* contemplation. *Umbrarum:* all those things which we explained before. *Corpora:* substances; *viva:* in pure liberty of knowledge and virtue. *Nephas:* illicit and impossible. *Carina:* body. *Vectare:* for the soul can scarcely live in the body in pure oblivion completely away from misery.

[392] *Alcidem:* Hercules descended to the underworld, but since he was a demigod, the return lay open to him, and he dragged the chained gatekeeper Cerberus with him. Hercules signifies the virtuous person, whence his names are appropriate. *Hercules* is *gloria litis,* "the glory of dispute." His labor makes him famous; thus Boethius: "Hard labors celebrate Hercules" (*Consolation,* bk. 4, meter 7. 13). And he is called *Alcides,* as if *fortis,* "strong,"

and *formosus*, "handsome." Strength denotes virtue, and beauty denotes glory. He descended to the underworld when by contemplation he came to temporal things, but since he was a demigod, rational and immortal in spirit, irrational and mortal in body, he returned from these things when he rose again to heavenly matters.

Cerberus is taken in the poetic fictions in two ways: for by him we understand the earth, whence his name is fitting. *Cerberus*, as if *caerberos*, that is, *carnem vorans*, "devouring the flesh." He consumes the flesh and leaves the bones. He has three heads: Europe, Asia, and Africa. Or he is triple headed because of his diverse qualities. He has something hot, very cold, and moderate; the Chaldeans believe that such are the three geographical zones. He is the doorkeeper in Orcus, since through him we enter the sublunary region. Fulgentius says Cerberus figures eloquence: *Cerberus* means "devouring the flesh"—eloquence penetrates and rebukes the carnal minds of listeners.[59] He is triple headed because he has the three principal disciplines—grammar, dialetic, and rhetoric—or because of the three types of legal pleading or poetry. He is the doorkeeper of Orcus. This *Orcus* has another meaning, because it figures the human body. Therefore Cerberus keeps the door because eloquence opens and closes the instrument of the mouth. Hercules drags out the chained Cerberus when he comprehends eloquence in precepts and other rules.

[393] Theseus indeed signifies wisdom; Pirithous, eloquence. These two companions are linked in love because, as Cicero says, these two types love to be joined: the wise person, if he is not eloquent, is held to be useful to himself alone, and the eloquent person, if he is not wise, is held to be useless and dangerous to his country. Martianus openly acknowledges the connection of these two when he introduces Mercury wanting to marry Philology.[60] Since, however, we read that Theseus was partly a mortal and partly a god, we take him to be wisdom, which is divine in its theoretic part and human in its practical part. And thus his name is fitting: Theseus is called *deus bonus:* "the good god."—*theos* is *deus*, "god," and *eu* is *bonum*, "good." He is called a god because of the theoretical knowledge of the divine, and he is called good because of the practical knowledge which teaches the human good, that is, the honest life. For integrity is the greatest good in life.

Pirithous is called the god of circumlocution: for *peri* is *circum*, "round about," and *theos* is *deus*, "god." By circumlocutions we understand nothing if not those wandering merchants who are eminently eloquent. Whence Mercury is so called as if *mercatorum kirios*, that is, "the god of merchants." Pirithous is said to be entirely mortal, because deeds remain and words are transient: both because speech concerns men alone and because after one speaks, speech does not remain. But wisdom remains and is immortal. Theseus and Pirithous descend to the underworld to carry off Proserpina. When merchants learn the course of the sun and moon and the natures of stars, they love to philosophize about mundane matters, but their "wisdom" drives out true wisdom. Indeed, their garrulity greatly defeats true eloquence.

[392–402] *Non sum letatus:* Charon was displeased because Hercules contemplated only out of curiosity. *Lacu:* Acheron, in which there are many contemplations. *Manu:* in work, in writing songs. *Solio:* in the seat of the soul, namely, the heart. *Trementem:* giving the gesture of trembling. Or *trementem:* since the accuser makes the accused tremble. *Fata:* the Sibyl. *Insidie:* the studies of curiosity. *Vim:* reason acts violently when it philosophizes because of curiosity only. *Antro:* by the movement of the throat, the trumpet of the chest. *Latrans:* by disputations and declamations. *Umbras:* the accused. *Casta:* a thought or oath not understood. *Patrui:* for she is the daughter of Pluto's brother Jove, that is, of the superior fire. *Limen:* the lunar circle which is the highest limit of the sublunary region.

[405–9] *Nulla:* Charon is not persuaded, because sometimes an old, wise person is displeased to see another philosophizing: because the elder knows the Creator, he fears that the young person lacks that wisdom, and therefore Sibyl shows the branch (*aperit ramum*) to Charon. *Veste:* good works by which people obscure their shameful vices, as with a robe. Or we say Aeneas's robe is the body under which the branch is hidden, since wisdom is hidden—that is, obscured—by the flesh. *Visum:* from the very beginning of philosophizing.

[410–13] *Pupim:* the blind and passionate body. *Ceruleam:* lividness is the sign of passion in this matter. Charon turns (*vertit*) the boat to Aeneas when the time of discreet age makes the flesh yield to the rational spirit. *Ripe:* the boat approaches the bank so that it may receive Aeneas, just as the flesh begins to endure annoying passions so that it may yield to the spirit. *Iuga:* joys. *Sedebant:* they delayed. *Deturbat:* Charon clears out those people seated on the ship's benches, just as an old man disparages those tarrying in pleasures. *Laxat:* Charon lets down the gangway of the boat when the time of discreet age controls the instruments of the senses. At the same time (*simul*) he accepts Aeneas (*Eneam accipit*) into the ship when he makes the flesh obey the spirit. For thus the ship sustains Aeneas when the flesh yields to the spirit. *Ingentem:* Aeneas is "massive" in comparison to the ship. For the spirit is greater than the body, and thus no corporeal good is able to fill it. *Gemuit:* the ship groans because of Aeneas's heaviness whenever the flesh cries out at the arduousness of the spirit's virtues.

[414–16] *Paludem:* the ship draws in the water of Acheron through chinks when the flesh admits the waves of annoying passion through the openings of the senses and the pores. *Tandem trans fluvium exponit:* after a long time Charon takes them across the waters—he bears them across the annoyances of the active life into the quiet life. *Limo:* in the quiet life of the purged person; for mud is watered earth. The philosophical life has the solidity of virtue and the moisture of instruction. And just as from the watered earth much fruit comes forth, so too from that philosophical life comes great utility. *Informi:* for philosophical life is not adorned by these corruptible ornaments. *In ulva:* sedge coming from mud is the moisture or greenness of deeds and virtue coming from such a life.

[417–23] *Regna:* as if in such life virtues command. *Personat:* Cerberus rebukes, for he especially urges the good. *Antro:* the caves in which Cerberus is kept are the profound arts in which eloquence is contained. *Adverso:* since these arts have makers who are adversaries: rhetoric has the accuser and the defender, and dialectic has the opponent and the respondent. The necks (*colla*) of Cerberus are the instruments with which he works. *Colubris:* with sharp and harmful words. Eloquence is like this when it lacks wisdom, and therefore *proicit offam melle:* "the Sibyl throws him a honey cake"—knowledge refreshes his soul with the sweetness of wisdom which, as the psalmist states, "is sweeter than honey or the honey comb."[61] *Frugibus medicatis:* with the uses of wisdom which heal error and vice. *Fame:* with the desire of knowing. *Tria . . . terga resolvit humi fusus:* Cerberus, now humbled, redirects the vigor of speaking through grammar, dialectic, and rhetoric toward solid and fruitful virtue—when eloquence receives wisdom, it is disposed to examine the teachings of wisdom about virtue. *Extenditur:* it is increased or expanded. When eloquence receives great wisdom, eloquence increases. *Antro:* the arts.

[424] *Aditum:* heart. Carefully note the order: for first the Sibyl fills Cerberus with the cake, and then Aeneas gains the entrance (*aditum occupat*), because first understanding joins wisdom to eloquence, and then the rational spirit begins to have the instruments of speech for teaching. For then the rational spirit begins to teach by offering eloquence which, joined to wisdom, teaches. For no one ought to claim the name of teacher before he possesses wisdom and eloquence. For if he presumes to teach and lacks either, he will lack both thought and discourse to explain the matter. If he has only wisdom, he knows what he should set forth, but he fails by being ignorant of how to explain skillfully what he knows. If, however, he has only the eloquence of a teacher, he knows how to speak, but he is ignorant of what he says. So one must prepare for the profession of teaching by joining wisdom and eloquence, and therefore Virgil says, "Aeneas begins the approach" (*aditum*). Aeneas forges on, having overcome the guardian (*custode sepulto*), that is, having enfolded eloquence in wisdom.

[425] *Evadit celer:* he goes across quickly, for he is talented and swift in comprehending things. *Ripam unde inremeabilis:* the bank of Acheron—the end of sorrow, "without return" because the person who once goes through the annoying, unsettled life returns unwillingly through it since he remembers the harshness which he has endured.

[426–30] *Continuo:* after wisdom has been joined to eloquence and teaching and after the free spirit has come to the quiet life, then at last the spirit sees the fallen and transitory life and recognizes these calamities, and those are the heard cries (*audite vagitus*)—The dispositions of the foolish spirit. There are four states of mind of the foolish spirit: joy, or the affect derived from present good; hope of future good; sorrow from present evil; fear of future evil. Therefore there are two concerning good, two concerning evil: joy and hope concerning good, sorrow and fear concerning evil; two concerning the present: joy and sorrow; and two concerning the future: hope and fear. Boethius notes these four:

Banish joy, banish fear,
Flee from hope, let not sorrow be present, etc.
[*Consolation*, bk. 1, meter 7. 25–28]

And Horace says:
Whether one rejoices or mourns, desires or fears—what difference does it make? [*Epistles*, 1. 6. 12]
The "voices" therefore are figure of these emotions deriving from good, that is, joy and hope. For the voice (the vocal outburst, for so we take the voice) is a sign of these emotions. *Vagitus*, "crying," is a sign of the other two, and therefore it signifies them. *Infantum:* we interpret infants as beginners in learning. *Limen:* the threshhold of knowledge. *Dulcis vite:* of the free spirit in knowledge and virtue. *Ubere:* doctrine by which beginners draw nourishment from the advanced. For teaching is the dissemination of knowledge. *Atra dies:* wicked desire. *Funere:* in the oppression of vice. *Iuxta:* cohabitors. *Dampnati:* infamous persons; *crimine:* disgrace; *mortis:* of vice; *falso:* for fame "sings of truth and fiction."[62]

[431] *Nec:* he notes the two types of those living in this temporal life: the weak and the infamous; and you should note those who make judgments about them. You read that there were three sons of Jove who are judges in the underworld: Minos, Rhadamanthus, and Aeacus. We take these as the three sole goods which we should possess: virtue, wisdom, and eloquence. These three have their origin in the Creator because they are good. Minos is so called because *Minos* in Greek is *clarus*, "bright," in Latin, and *mene* is *clara*, "bright." Interpret Minos as wisdom which illumines the spirit; Rhadamanthus as eloquence. For Rhadamanthus is so called because *Radamantus* in Greek is *iudicans verbum*, "judging the word," in Latin. It is eloquence's task to judge the word: through grammar it eliminates errors of speech, through dialectic it distinguishes the true from the false, and through rhetoric it adorns speech with figures. Aeacus is so called as if *Heroachaos*, that is, *dominus confusionis*, "lord of confusion," since virtue rules over the confusion of vice. Therefore, Minos is the judge of the wise and mistaken, Rhadamanthus of the elo-

quent and the ineloquent, and Aeacus of the virtuous and the vicious. *Sorte:* disposition.

[432–33] *Urnam movet silentum concilium vocat:* Minos investigates the death—vice—of those killed by vices so that he may instruct those gathered together there. For it is the duty of the wise person to call many to his teaching, and he inquires so that he may correct by given laws what he has found out.

[434–37] *Proxima deinde:* he speaks sharply to the weak and the infamous. All evil persons are said to live together. Their cohabitation is the depraved life. *Sibi peperere letum manu:* to destroy oneself in vice with wicked works. He notes irresponsible persons. *Lucem:* wisdom; *proiecere:* to subdue by the pleasures of the body. *Ethere:* glittering with wisdom and divinity. *Pauperiem:* contempt for ephemeral good which philosophers (such as Diogenes) had.

[438–39] *Palus:* oblivion. *Stix:* hatred. *Novies:* there are nine kinds of hatred, namely the nine contempts for knowledge. To have contempt for the three disciplines of eloquence is a triple hatred and to despise the three of philosophical practice is a triple hatred, and to neglect the three of theory is a triple hatred. Therefore, Styx flows through nine riverbeds when hatred flows against the nine sciences. Styx nine times confines the interposed persons (*interfusa novies cohercet*), those wishing to return to the lost life, those seeking to be returned to forsaken learning, because hatred, excluding wisdom from them, prevents the nine sciences from working. He who desires to be wise ought to love the exercise of knowledge.

[440–44] *Nec:* after having noted the three types of persons living in this secular life which the rational spirit contemplates (namely, the weak, the infamous, and the irresponsible), Virgil notes the fourth—the lecherous life. And note that although Virgil designates other vices by men, he illustrates lechery through individual women alone, for the woman designates weakness and softness; here this vice is especially subject to weakness and softness. He notes diverse kinds of lechery with diverse examples. *Non procul hinc:* this vice is not very distant from those noted above, because they go together. *Lugentes:* the sins of lechery. By these names Virgil signifies the double nature of lechery. Lechery first offers a certain delight, but ultimately it burdens the spirit with the lamentations of penance and of bad conscience. So Boethius:

Like the flying bee: it fled from where it found pleasing honey and stung the hearts very fiercely. [*Consolation*, bk. 3, meter 7. 3–6]

Thus, as we said earlier, the Chimaera signifies lechery—at first sweet, then pungent. *Calles:* the paths leading to those fields are the vices which lead to loves, which Ovid shows are many in *The Art of Love* (1. 35): "In the beginning because you want to love, etc." *Secreti:* they are said to be hidden because, although they are evil, they are considered good when men pursue them because of courtliness.[63] *Mirthea:* of Venus; *silva:* the "groves" which are shady—ignorance indeed has that. *Tegit:* ignorance covers up. *Cure morte non relinquunt:* pains accompany that vices's oppression. Or, interpret it differently in terms of the other death. *Cure:* imaginary reconsiderations, namely, illusions. *Non relinquunt:* in mortification of the flesh, we cannot immediately be purged of these illusions.

[445–47] *Phedram:* in the case of Phaedra understand a certain kind of lechery which is called "incest," namely "loving unlawfully." *Procrin:* Procris is the class of jealous persons. *Euriphilem:* Eriphyle is the class of greedy lovers. *Evadnen:* Evadne was Capaneus's wife, who, having heard that he was dead, sought his body, and having found it, lay with and embraced it. Therefore, by her understand lovers so unrestrained that they do not know that death imposes an end of their love. *Pasiphen:* in Pasiphaë understand the class of lovers whose love violates the laws of nature. *Laodamia:* she is the class of lovers so degenerately obsessed with love that no necessity of food or sleep or drink or anything else offers a respite.

[448–49] *Iuvenis Ceneus:* Caeneus was first a woman, then she changed into the sex of a man, so then she was called Caeneus, although she before had been named Caenis; she was changed again into a woman and took back her first name. We said that the feminine sex signifies the frailty of vice; the male sex, however, signifies the strength of virtue. One changes from a woman into a man when one moves from the frailty of vice to the vigor of virtue. One reverts from man to woman when one backslides from the vigor of virtue to the weakness of vice, which you observe happening especially in lechery, as Terence says: Phaedria rose from femininity to manhood when he thought to leave the love of Thais; he relapsed, however, from manhood to femininity when he turned back from that honest undertaking to his first weakness.[64] Therefore Caeneus (or Caenis) is properly called the son or daughter of novelty, since she is suddenly changed to such diverse things. *Fato:* by temporal event.

[450–76] *Inter quas:* while Aeneas contemplates the various classes of passion, he sees his former passion in his imagination, and thus he sees the shade of Dido. *Recens a vulnere:* still fresh because she recently died. *Errabat silva:* "she wandered through the grove"—she returned in memory, in the pleasant shadow of love. *Stetit:* he paused to contemplate her, whom he had loved shamefully a short time ago. *Umbram:* reconsideration. *Obscuram qualem:* she did not seem so beautiful to him; just as the moon is at first shining, then hidden, and again resumes the flickering flame, so passion, which before flourished in beautiful visions and then died, now returns with weak remembrance. *Lacrimans:* Aeneas "weeps," repenting because he erred so shamefully. *Affatus:* Aeneas speaks to Dido's shade when the rational spirit contemplates the nature of passion through recollection. *Nuntius:* reason telling Aeneas that Dido has died is reason pointing out a spirit freed from slavery to passion and also teaching that passion has departed. *Ferro:* with the sharpness of rebuke. *Causa:* if he does not abandon passion, she will not depart. As long as we assent to passion, for that length of time we give it strength. And so it is said, "Go near the fire, and you'll get hotter" (Terence, *The Eunuch* 85). *Invitus:* for unless he fights with himself, he will never abandon passion. *Litore:* the end of passion. *Deum:* of knowledge and virtue. *Senta:* stinging. For just as sharp thorns draw blood from the body, so earthly goods by their pricking draw strength from the spirit. *Nec:* for he does not believe that passion which inheres with such fierce bonds will go away if he abandons it. *Siste:* Dido sees Aeneas and flees; this happens when the lecherous person does not pay attention to the wise man's learning. Aeneas calls the fleeing Dido to a conversation when the rational spirit calls the embarrassed lecherous person to instruction. *Teque:* Dido leaves the sight of Aeneas when the lecherous person seeks to hide from the wise man's knowledge. *Ardentem:*

To err is properly to burn. *Torva:* Dido truculently looks at Aeneas when the lecherous person puts up a strong defense against arming himself rationally. *Oculos:* Dido casts her eyes down when the lecherous person does not raise his wit and reason to celestial matters. *Incepto:* after evil has been undertaken. *Vultum:* desire, because desire shows in the face; thus Juvenal: You may detect the torment of the soul hidden in a sick body, and you may detect joy; the face shows whatever is held within [*Satires* 10. 18–19]

Sermone: a sermon is ethical instruction directed to those present. *Silex:* for just as flint is immobile and dumb, so lechery is stupid and irresponsible. *Tandem:* after Aeneas contemplates Dido, she fades from his memory. *Corripuit in nemus:* she fades or vanishes into the pleasing shadow of her ignorance. Dido sees *Sicheus* as a spiritual good—which we know as the vices of gluttony and intoxication—and the Epicureans claim the soul can have no greater good. He is Dido's husband, because lechery rejoices with gluttony: "Venus grows cold without Ceres and Bacchus."[65] *Equat:* for just as gluttony loves lechery, lechery equally loves gluttony. Neither is satisfied without the other. *Casu percussus:* death; Aeneas is moved by her fate. He is not yet of such perfection that he is not moved by the departure of what pleased him. Thus he pushes on (*prosequitur, etc.*): he returns to contemplation of images in memory.

[477–88] *Iter:* contemplation, which is the route from creatures to the Creator. *Arva ultima:* the army's duty, which is the defense of others, and therefore called *ultima*, as if the foundation of others. *Secreta:* separated from other duties. You read in the *Timaeus* that this duty is thus separated from the others so that never will anyone join anything else to this duty. Thus Plato: "One tax is levied for protecting the state; this tax is imposed on all and is properly given only to those persons who will wage war for the safety of all" (*Timaeus* 17D). *Occurrit:* Tydeus appears. Aeneas notes the diverse kinds of men engaged in military matters. Interpret Tydeus as those having strength greater than the size of their bodies. For in Tydeus "the greater strength ruled in a small body." In Parthenopaeus understand those whose strength exceeds youthful prowess. In Adrastus, those whose strength conquers the weakness of age; Aeneas notes these men in Adrastus. *Ad superos:* rational persons who acknowledge their errors. *Caduci:* "the fallen," the backsliders into vice. *Dardanide:* those who wish to defend the body (by which we understand Troy) against vice. *Quos:* those engaged in drilling the army; *cernens:* discovering errors with eyes of contemplation. *Glaucum:* in these three men—Glaucus, Medon, and Tersilochus—see the three ways of defending the republic. For there are three kinds of war: national, when men of the same or different countries fight; civil, when men within the same state fight; more than civil war, when men of the same family fight. Plato notes these three types of hostility in the *Timaeus* (17D) where he says: the duty of the army is to protect the state against external, internal, and domestic enemies. Joined to these, therefore, are the three kinds of war: against external, internal, and domestic enemies. Therefore, enemies are called *Antenorides*, "those set against." *Poliboeten:* interpret him as those people who do not respect the dignity of their holy authority. *Ideum:* Paris was nurtured in Ida. Interpret him as those who do not consider the undoing of their country when they inflict injury on someone. *Circumstant frequentes dextra:* those who remain in these military duties, that is, those who are active in good work. *Vidisse:* to look with the eyes of contemplation. *Morari:* to linger by investigating their errors or good works. *Et conferre:* Aeneas journeys with them when he turns his contemplation to their deeds. *Causas veniendi:* purposes for which they are born.

[489–93] *At Danaum:* we say that the Greeks attacking Troy are vices or bodily necessities vexing the body. Agamemnon, who commands the Greeks, is reason placed above vices and necessities. Thus his name is appropriate. He is called Agamemnon as if *agonis mene,* that is, *certaminis claritas,* "clarity of argument." Reason illumines the virtues oppressing the vices. Agamemnon has a brother Menelaus—virtue; he is called Menelaus as if *clara,* "bright," and *lapidea,* "rocklike"; for *mene* is *claritas,* "brightness," and *laos* is *lapis,* "stone." Indeed, virtue, because it is practised, is therefore bright; because it is arduous, it is stonelike. Therefore, *proceres Danaum,* "the Greek princes," are those of many vices. They do not await Aeneas's arrival, because they fear rational conversation. *Agamemnonie falanges:* Agamemnon's legions are the multitudes of vices which Agamemnon rules since reason has power over vices. *Arma:* the exercise of bright reason. *Umbras:* temporal goods. *Pars:* the frightened Greeks flee Aeneas when sinful persons do not heed the censure of the rational person. *Exiguam vocem tollunt:* "the Greeks shout weakly" when vices conduct a weak defense. *Ceu:* Aeneas forces the Greeks back to their ships when the rational person makes the sinful look at their wicked desires, and he forces them to enter the ships, that is, punishes their wicked desires. *Clamor frustratur:* their defense fails.

[494–97] *Atque hic:* one reads that Helen was first married to Menelaus, from whom Paris seized her and married her. After Menelaus killed Paris, Helen married Deiphobus, who was Priam's son and Paris's brother. After the city was captured, Menelaus attacked Deiphobus and cut off his hands, feet, ears, and nose and put out his eyes. Aeneas sees his butchered body. We have said that Menelaus is virtue bright with reason and rocklike with endurance. Helen, however, is so called as if *helenne*, that is, *dea inhabitans*, "goddess residing." *Hel* is *dea*, "goddess," and *enne* is *inhabitans*, "residing." This is earthly riches because it dwells and rules on earth. She is said to have been the most beautiful woman because she was thought more worth seeking than other goods. Therefore, Helen was first given to Menelaus because earthly riches were first made to serve virtue, but she was seized by Paris, when she turns from the virtuous to the sensual man. For *Paris* in Greek is *sensus*, "sense," in Latin, as we have said. Therefore, after Helen forgot Menelaus, she chose Paris, because after earthly riches abandon the virtuous man, they give themselves up to the sensual man. Thus philosophers show that earthly wealth is bad because it frequently joins with evil. After Helen marries Paris, the Greeks wage war against Troy—after wealth joins with the sensual person, vices begin to attack the body. For vices especially attack the body when they discover wealth, which is their opportunity. Therefore, wise men set about to abandon wealth so that we may seek to be free of vice. Finally, Menelaus kills Paris when virtue mortifies sensuality. Then Helen clings to Deiphobus since, after the mortification of sense, wealth offers itself to the timorous man. He is called Deiphobus as if *dimophobus*, that is, *terror publicus*, "public fear."[66] Priam is so called as if *iperamus*, that is, *superior pressura*, "greater force." By him we understand the passion which, rising at the moment of birth, sustains the life of the body for a whole lifetime, and therefore one reads that he reigned in Troy. He is said to be an old man since (as we have said before) that age has the greatest miseries. Priam therefore begot Paris and Deiphobus, since passion (as had been said often) produces sense and fear. Therefore, after Paris dies, Helen is given to Deiphobus because, after sense is mortified, opulence yields to fear when it is possessed by a person who, giving up sensual things, fears that he will not find anything greater. The Greeks take the city when the body yields to vice. Menelaus attacks Deiphobus because virtue attacks fear. He cuts off Deiphobus's hands and feet when he shows that Deiphobus lacks prudence in ways and means. Menelaus blinds Deiphobus and cuts off his ears when he shows him that he does not know those things which he should see and hear. Aeneas sees Deiphobus in the underworld without hands, feet, eyes, and ears, since the rational spirit contemplates fear, which is ignorant of what to do, where to go, what to listen to, or what to see, and because fear is greatly chastised in the army. Thus, he (*hic*) is said to be in these arms, that is, in military duties. *Ora:* the senses of hearing, sight, smell, and taste. *Ambas:* good and evil work.

[498–514] *Vix agnovit:* Aeneas scarcely recognizes Deiphobus, since the rational spirit scarcely admits fear into itself—for thus it is said that not to know vice is to avoid it. *Tegentem:* although none of those mentioned above has prudence in him, nonetheless they pretend to. *Compellat:* Aeneas questions Deiphobus when the rational spirit discerns perturbation about these things. *Notis:* Deiphobus knows Aeneas's voice because the fearful spirit often takes instruction from the rational man; because the fearful person never fulfills what the rational man advises, he is therefore repeatedly instructed so that he at some time will fulfill what the rational spirit constantly advises. If ever he does what he is commanded, then he will be ordered to advance no farther. *Ultro:* the terrified spirit does not seek instruction from the rational spirit. *Armipotens:* Deiphobus puts armed persons to flight. *Teucri:* all Trojans have their origin in Teucer, whose name comes from *Theucrus,* as if *theos cronon,* that is, *deus temporis,* "the god of time." The god of time is the sun, which by its coming gives summer; by its leaving, winter; by its rising and setting, day and night. Therefore, Troy and the Trojans have their origin in Teucer, since by the sun the body and its nature flourish. *Fama:* rumor says that Deiphobus dies when the instruction of reason teaches that the terrified spirit has withdrawn from virtue. *Nocte:* ignorance. *Cede:* mortification of vice. *Tumulum:* envelopment in oblivion. *Retheo:* Rhoeteum is so called from *retheos,* as if *resis theos,* which in Latin is *eloquentie deus,* "the god of eloquence." The god of eloquence is philosophy, which both shows what we should say and also restrains eloquence from insolent garrulity. Therefore, Deiphobus is buried on the Rhoetean shore (*Retheo litore*), since, in the beginning of philosophizing, fear is covered in oblivion. *Manes:* infernal spirits. Aeneas calls (*vocat*) loudly to the infernal spirits when the rational spirit invites those yearning for temporal goods to its great instruction. *Locum:* oblivion. *Arma:* the arms with which Deiphobus fights are the rumors with which fear terrorizes us. *Amice:* Aeneas esteems Deiphobus, because the rational spirit instructs the terrified spirit. *Conspicere:* the descending Aeneas cannot see Deiphobus, because the rational spirit forsaking corporeal goods cannot feel fear. If the imprudent person sets about to move from visible to invisible matters, he is greatly terrified because he does not believe that he is about to discover things better than those he has forsaken. *Terra:* solid and fruitful virtue. Aeneas cannot bury Deiphobus in his native country, that is, he cannot number fear among the heavenly virtues. *Atque hec:* Deiphobus answers Aeneas when the nature of fear is evident to the rational spirit. *Solvisti:* Aeneas is obligated to bury Deiphobus, since it is reasonable for the rational spirit to assign fear to oblivion. *Umbris:* transitory goods. *Fata:* temporal events. *Lacene* is interpreted as if *laceneos,* that is, *latens novitas,* "newness lying hidden." Helen is called Laconian since, because of wealth, new things are hidden away. In order to have wealth we hold back recently acquired things. *His:* Helen brings that evil to Deiphobus, because wealth makes a person fearful and indiscreet. And when the terrified person is commanded to forsake his accustomed temporal wealth, he therefore ignores what he ought to do. *Supremam noctem:* greatest ignorance; *egerimus:* we Trojans, that is, carnal persons. *Necesse:* inevitable. The rational spirit need not be wary unless it recalls the pleasure of past life.

[515–16] *Cum fatalis:* Troy was destroyed (as we know) by a horse. The horse, enclosing many Greeks, was taken into the city, and, when the Trojans were asleep, the horse released the hidden Greeks into the city. In poetic fictions the horse has two figures; it signifies the will, as in Horace: "You, a wise person, release in time the aging horse, etc." (*Epistles* 1. 1. 8). And therefore the horse because of its speed figures new desire, because it quickly changes its course. The horse also signifies lechery as in the story of Diomedes feeding his guests to his horses (the lecherous person subjecting his familiar friends to his lechery). The horse has this meaning because in this animal lechery flourishes especially. Pliny in his book about natural history says that mares are so unrestrained in passion that, when they cannot find males, they go to the mountain peaks and there are impregnated by the breath of the winds.[67] In this manner the swiftest horses bring forth young, but they do not live long. Here the Trojan horse is also a figure of lechery. The horse holds an infinite number of Greeks, since lechery contains various vices such as incest, adultery, fornication, and harlotry, which subdivide into other kinds of vice. The Greeks made the horse, since the drunkenness and gluttony of lechery are in Troy, according to that saying: "Venus grows cold without Ceres and Bacchus."[68] The Trojans sleep when they do not exercise knowledge and virtue, and then the horse releases the Greeks whom it contains, since lechery brings forth from itself diverse kinds of vice. When the exercise of virtue is halted, wantonness, prodigality, and avarice come forth from lechery. But how prodigality and avarice can both come from lechery when they are contraries deserves consideration. The person who labors in lechery sees that he lacks much which he will have to spend on lechery, and therefore he searches with a great effort so that he may abound in these things; he is miserly with the use of what he has attained, and thus lechery produces avarice. Prodigality in this case is sufficiently obvious: the lover, satisfying his whore and also his go-betweens, gives away everything. From lechery also come inertia, irresponsibility, sloth, laziness, idleness, and inconstancy, whose definitions we give briefly so that we may set forth their nature. Lechery is a vice which urges us to satisfy the troublesome suggestions of bodily desire. Wantonness goads passion by exceeding the moderate use of bodily dress and other furnishings. Prodigality irresponsibly seeks money and the immoderate expending of it. Avarice violently heaps up money and insatiably craves it. Inertia is ignorance of all of the arts, both liberal and mechanical. Thus we say that those whom we see living without art have no inheritance. Irresponsibility is the vice by which someone scorns the exercise of his art and profession. Sloth is the stiffness and slowness of the body which dreads the undertaking of honest duty. Laziness is the disuse of study and of any appropriate act. Idleness is desisting totally from nearly every care, study, or labor. Inconstancy is fickleness of mind about various endeavors. The Greeks are smuggled into the city and set it in flames when vice overcomes the body with the heat of its burning after the flesh consents to vice. *Fatalis:* mortal. *Saltu supervenit Pergama:* the horse leaping over Troy is passion oppressing the body with a sudden goad. And lest you think this to mean the body of animals (this has nothing to do with animals), the text notes that the heights (*ardua*) are overcome; indeed, the bodies of animals are prone on the earth. *Gravis:* for lechery is lazy and indolent. *Peditem:* vice, because it crawls among the lowest things. *Alvo:* moderation.

[517–27] *Illa:* Helen—wealth. *Simulans chorum:* exultation. *Orgia:* the feasts of Bacchus. *Orge* in Greek is *colere,* "to worship": whence those feasts are called orgies antonomastically, since they were first celebrated thrice annually or triennially. Whence they are also called *triatherica.* It is correct to say that Helen celebrated the feasts of Bacchus, since wealth usually spurs drunkards. Properly also, she led the Phrygian women (*Frigias*) around the horse, since wealth entangles carnal men in lechery. The Trojan women are carnal and weak. *Media:* Helen is in the midst of the Trojans, since among carnal men wealth is go-between. *Flammam:* the fire of wicked suggestion. *Summa:* Helen calls the Greeks to destroy the city when wealth incites vice to subvert and conquer the spirit with the flesh. And then she holds the citadel (*arcem*), since when the citadel is controlled she then holds the heights of power. *Confectum curis:* the fearful person is tormented with anxieties of fear. *Somno:* laziness in the exercise of virtue. *Talamus infelix:* Deiphobus is wretched in his chamber because of the attacking Greeks—the wicked mind fears the attacks of vice in the flesh and becomes desperate (*pressit*). *Arma amovet:* Helen removes the arms from the walls when wealth takes the exercise of the powers and judgments of the spirit from the mind. *Fidum ensem capiti:* "and she removes the faithful sword from under Deiphobus's head"—wealth distracts the mind of the fearful person from nature. *Interea . . . intra tecta:* "meanwhile within the walls" she calls Menelaus to kill Deiphobus—wealth invites virtue into the mind to mortify fear. *Limina pandit:* "she opens the doors" when wealth opens the senses. Wealth disposes our senses to virtue, because virtue understands our senses in such matters because it sees them clinging to wealth. *Amanti:* Menelaus wished Helen to be his wife again, since virtue desires wealth to yield to it. When Deiphobus is dead, Helen thinks she will satisfy Menelaus: after fear is extinguished, wealth thinks it will please the virtuous person. Nevertheless, the virtuous person hates wealth, since he sees it joined to fear, and thus Menelaus hated Helen since she was joined to Deiphobus. *Et famam:* after Deiphobus died, Helen's disgrace was blotted out; after fear is mortified, wealth is no longer disgraceful. Wealth had been accused since it made man so fearful that he was not able to gaze at the heavens.

[528–47] *Irrumpunt:* Menelaus and Ulysses burst in—virtue and wisdom (as we interpret Menelaus and Ulysses) enter the mind. *Scelerum:* for the vicious man thinks it a crime when anyone denies him his vice. *Eolides:* Ulysses had his origin in Aeolus, because all knowledge has its beginnings in glory. Thus we said before that the fount of the Muses flowed from the hoof mark of the horse Pegasus. *Grais:* Menelaus and Ulysses. *Dii:* divine dispositions. *Talia:* so that they might be mortified. For the fearful person sees that he is beset by knowledge and virtue, and he therefore wishes them dead. *Sed te:* Deiphobus speaks to Aeneas when the fearful person wonders at the rational spirit. *Erroribus pelagi:* in the vices of the flesh. *Divum:* of knowledge and virtue. *Venis:* you, Aeneas, descend to temporal matters through contemplation. *Fortuna:* fate, namely divine command. *Domos:* temporal goods. *Sole:* with the splendor of knowledge and the warmth of vigor of virtue. *Hac vice:* when Aeneas and Deiphobus are speaking, the sunrise (*aurora*) occurs—when the rational spirit inquires about and knows the properties of the fearful, the latter's mind begins to be illuminated. Here sunrise is the first glittering of knowledge shining in the eyes of the human mind. *Traiecerat axem medium:* sunrise penetrates the heart of man; this is done *eterio,* by a divine advent. *Et fors:* the spirit never relinquishes fear unless understanding leads it beyond fear. *Admonuit:* what the Sibyl says to Aeneas is given above. We will not repeat these and entirely similar matters, or we shall not have time for matters not yet discussed. *Nox ruit:* temporal life which passes through the tumbling succession of moments. *Flendo:* the rational and understanding person seeing this life mourns that it is nothing but a postponement of living. *Hic:* in temporal life. *Ambas:* virtue and vice. *Via:* human conversion. *Dextra:* virtue. *Menia:* we have already spoken about the walls. *Tendit:* one approaches by contemplation. *Elisium:* you should know that the underworld is divided into two parts, Tartarus and Elysium, which signify on earth the life of the virtuous and the life of the sinful. The good life is called *Elysium,* from *eleison,* that is, *locus misericordie et claritudinis,* "the place of mercy and splendor," and the life of the wicked is called Tartarus, that is, *Infernus,* as if "inferior." The right road leads to Elysium, the left to Tartarus, since virtue in the good life and vice in the bad locate their followers. *Penas:* the torments of the penance of anxiety and of wicked conscience. *Contra Deiphebus:* Deiphobus answers the Sibyl when the natural property of fear is exposed to understanding. *Sevi:* the Sibyl is said to rage when understanding, ever so justly, becomes fiercely angry against vice. *Explebo . . . tenebris:* "I will return to darkness," that is, to foolish ignorance. *I:* "go," Aeneas, to contemplation; *nostrum:* human. *Tantum . . . vestigia torsit:* Deiphobus in speaking turns his steps because the fearful person flees when he is exposed to understanding.

[548–53] *Respicit:* when fear departs, Aeneas considers it with the eyes of contemplation. *Lata menia:* "the broad walled city" of great Dis, located under a cliff and encircled with a triple wall (*circumdata triplici muro sub rupe*); the walled city is the five kinds of temporal goods—sufficiency, power, dignity, glory, delight. It is called "great Dis" since temporal goods are earthly. It is encircled with a triple wall, because it is enclosed by ignorance, poverty, and weakness. It is located beneath a cliff, that is, situated under bad fortune; it is broad (*lata*)—it is fit for error and digression.[69] *Flegeton:* the ardor of the angry. *Saxa:* the types of weapons. *Porta:* fraud through which these earthly goods enter.

The adamantine pillars (*columpne*) in these walls are the previously mentioned affects of the soul which cannot be uprooted: joy, sorrow, hope, fear. *Adamante:* the eternal remorse of the heart. *Vis . . . virum:* the power of the virtuous. *Celicole:* the spirit. *Excindere:* to root out with iron (*ferro*)—with teaching which cuts off useless things with the sharp edge of rebuke.

[554–56] *Stat . . . turris ad auras:* the tower here raised up high is the lofty mind "looking" (as you know) at the air, that is, gaping at temporal goods. *Thesiphone succincta cruenta palla:* wicked speech attended by quarrelling. *Vestibulum:* the gateway by which one leaves the tower is the wicked mouth, the passage away from the exalted mind, and Tisiphone properly guards (*servat*) this. *Insopnis:* restless and implacable. *Noctes:* knowledge or ignorance can assist the exalted mind, but wise men rise higher by distinguished deeds than do foolish men by wicked deeds. Evil speech always has a place in the wicked mouth of the proud person.

[557–77] *Hinc:* from these temporal goods. *Gemitus:* the complaints of those when they are taken away. *Verbera:* the punishments of thieves. *Strepitum . . . hausit:* Aeneas understands this cacophony. *Facies:* he asks about the kind of crime. *Ad auras:* they weep because of temporal goods. *Casto:* pure of vice. *Limen:* the previously mentioned gateway. *Deum penas:* that is, punishment imposed by the gods, by divine ideas. *Gnosius:* because eloquence flourished in Crete. *Habet:* only in these realms is eloquence exercised. *Superos:* that is, those who did not repent while still alive. *Mortem:* the oppression of vice. *Ultrix:* Tisiphone, "the avenger," because she punishes crimes with rebukes. *Accincta:* completely armed with the whip (*flagello*) of reproach. *Sinistra:* with false accusation—for Tisiphone's right hand is true accusation. *Anguis:* poisonous and harsh words. *Vocat:* Tisiphone calls her sisters when wicked speech excites both wicked thoughts and wicked deeds. *Panduntur:* the terrible doors open when mouths of the wicked are opened to answer rebukes. *Custodia:* Tisiphone. *Ydra:* ignorance itself. *Hiatibus:* with infinite questions. *Sevior:* for ignorance in the heart is worse than wicked speech in the mouth. *Intus:* in that mind.

[578–79] *Bis in preceps Tartarus patet:* "Tartarus stretches out twice as far . . ."—the wretched life has two pitfalls—it burdens the flesh with troubles and weighs down the spirit with vice, according to that passage from Horace:

This body, burdened with vices, at the same time burdens the spirit and casts a bit of divine breath to earth.[70]

Tendit sub auras: the evil life pushes down its followers under fallen goods. *Suspectus:* beyond the visible to Olympus (*ad . . . Olimpum*), that is, to theology. This is the meaning here: as much as the wise person in taking up divine matters transcends temporal goods, to the same extent does the wicked life push down its followers beneath those same temporal goods.

[580–84] *Hic:* in this walled city; allegorically it signifies the pain by which the followers of the five temporal goods are punished. Now Virgil shows the kinds of followers and their punishments. *Antiquum:* the sons of Titan and Earth—the Giants—human bodies made from the sun and earth. *Fulmine:* divine power. *In imo:* in the lower order of creatures, as we said, when we earlier discussed the places of the underworld. *Aloidas:* the sons of Aloeus grew taller daily. *Aloe* in Greek is *amaritudo*, "bitterness," in Latin: *Aloeus*, in Greek is interpreted as *amarus*, "bitter." Aloeus therefore is understood as the bitter man whom we know to be greedy. For what greater bitterness is there than to watch day and night in great fear, to be terrified of wicked thieves, fires, and servants? What is a greater bitterness than to torment the flesh with labors and not to assuage the torment with any sustenance? Aloeus begets his two sons when the greedy person produces cupidity and abundance. These two grow daily when greater abundance repays desire and desire is enflamed by greater abundance, according to that passage from Ovid: "The more they drink the more they thirst" (*Fasti* 1. 216), and according to that passage from Juvenal: "Love of money grows however much that money increases" (*Satires* 14. 139). These two sons of Aloeus wish to drive Jove (*Iovem*) from his throne when cupidity and abundance seek to drive the soul from the divinity of knowledge and virtue. Jupiter is to be taken, as we said before, in diverse ways. As the superior fire, whence it is said, "From Jove, the origin of the Muses." As the spirit of the world, whence it is said, "Everything is filled with Jove." As the planet, whence, after Saturn, Jupiter is said to be first in the order of the planets. As the Creator, whence he is called "ominipotent Jupiter."[71] As the human soul in this poetic fiction. And according to this interpretation we say first the world, since it is ruled by Jove, and then man, who is moved by the soul. Thus man is called Microcosmus, the lesser world. In this world, heaven is the divine nature of the spirit from which the Aloides wish to cast out Jove.

[585–92] *Salmonea:* we read that Salmoneus reigned in Elis and was so much Jove's rival that he made for himself his own world having the four elements, lightning, thunder, and clouds. He signifies the tyrant and is so named: Salmoneus as if *salmoneos*, that is, *illator novitatis*, "the bringer of novelty." The tyrant brings novelty to us when he represents himself having divine power transcending the human. Indeed, the region is called *Elis, Eleydam*, "Elisian," that is, having the form of divine work which is the republic. The divine work, however, is the world, and the republic shares its form and thus is called another world. Just as the world has four regions, and each has its own adornment, so the city is divided into four areas by politicians; and just as in the highest region are the rational substances and in the lowest region are the brutes, likewise in the city. The philosophers Plato and Socrates are in the citadel, the soldiers are in the second quarter, the merchants are in the third, and the farmers are in the suburbs. This, therefore, is the world of Salmoneus. Lightning and thunder and clouds are the arms, trumpets, and battles. The shining and glittering arms are lightning. The blare of the trumpet and horn is the crash of thunder, and the throng of arrows in battle is rain. And just as thunder warns of rain and lightning, so that other noise warns of wars and arms. *Nubila:* the clouds cast up by Salmoneus are ignorance swirling around the tyrant. *Telum:* adverse fortune.

[595–600] *Necnon:* it is said that Tityus raped Latona, whence in the underworld he endures the punishment of vultures perpetually gnawing his liver. He represents the curious person, and he even sounds the very word in his name. He is called Tityus as if *tisiceos*, that is, *consumptus anima*, "consumed in spirit"; *tisis* is *consumptio*, "consumption," *scea* is *umbra* or *anima*, "shade" or "spirit." For the curious person is consumed in spirit since, when he searches vehemently for the arcane nature of things by laborious study, he consumes his mind insofar as its immortal nature permits. Latona, the mother of Apollo, is instruction producing wisdom. Whence Latona is so called as if *latitona,* "speaking the hidden," since instruction lies hidden. Tityus therefore wishes to join himself to Latona when the curious person wishes to grasp instruction. And therefore his liver is given to vultures in the underworld since, while he is alive, his mind is oppressed by the sharp anxieties of study. *Alumpnum:* for the curious person when he lazily philosophizes is fed by the fruits of the earth which he does not cultivate, according to Juvenal: "When sated Horace says 'euhoe' " (*Satires* 7. 62). The nine acres (*novem iugera*) are the nine sciences: three each of eloquence, theory, and practice. *Corpus:* the substance of anything. Substance is spirit. *Rostro:* bite. *Vultur:* anxiety. *Adunco:* fierce. *Fibris:* minds. *Renatis:* the mind is said to be reborn, since, although the mind is eaten by constant anxiety, what is consumed nevertheless survives.

[601–3] *Ixiona:* we said Ixion is to be interpreted as *super omnia,* "above all things," and he is to be taken here as a figure of the sun. Indeed, he signifies a judge, which is figured forth by this word because, when judgment is expected by the accuser, defender, and audience, he is placed above all in veneration. *Piritous:* as we said before, Pirithous is the exhorter, judge, and orator. *Laphite* are so called as if *laophite,* stony and fiery—when they ever so minimally spare criminals and even supplicants and incite themselves against such people with flames of anger, judges rightly are called stony and fiery. *Laos* is *lapis,* "stone," and *pheton* is *ardor,* "heat." *Silex* is the blow of fortune. *Imminet:* those who hold offices always fear (as Dionysius the Sicilian king knew) the blow of threatening fortune. The thrones gleam (*lucent*); the previously mentioned Dionysius fashioned ornate furnishings of purple for his throne.

[605–7] *Maxima:* the greatest in wickedness is Megaera—evil deed is more iniquitous than evil speech and evil thought. *Acubat:* Megaera lurks in their conscience, which is signified by *thorum:* "the couch." For *accubare* is *in thoro iacere,* "to lie on the couch." *Prohibet:* Megaera forbids—when wicked deed reaccuses through memory and denies the body any rest, the spirit is greatly saddened. *Facem:* anger. But when memory returns through recollection, the spirit knows itself to be the villain and greatly excites itself with anger against itself. *Intonat:* it threatens punishment. *Ore:* by reason, which speaks eloquently and which should punish offenses. When a wicked deed recurs in the mind, reason lodges a complaint in which conscience accuses desire: reason is the judge, fear imprisons, and remorse inflicts the penalty.

[608–14] *Hic:* in these fields, namely in the life of evil persons. We said that one interprets this walled city as the five kinds of temporal goods. And therefore it is easy to see why the Giants, the Aloides, Salmoneus, Tityus, and the Lapithae are said to be there. The Giants are in one of those houses since our bodies are indeed enslaved in desire. The Aloides dwell in temporal sufficiency, Salmoneus in power, the Lapithae in dignity, Tityus in glory. *Fratres:* companions in duties and discipline. Hatred among brothers occurs in this life when people envy their colleagues in disciplines who flourish in knowledge. They who strike their father *(patrem pulsant)* are those who rebuke their teacher. This is a very grievous offense indeed! *Fraus:* in the narratives, dependents are the members of the body since they serve the soul. One therefore defrauds dependents when he leads the members of his own body to error. The flesh knows nothing by itself, and therefore the soul deceives the flesh when the soul lures an imprudent person to what it sees to be evil. *Suis:* those close kin. The avaricious person "wishes to give nothing to his poor friend by which he might dispel cold and heavy hunger."[72] *Ob adulterium:* allegorically we understand wives to be duties. Thus one is taught that he should not be without a wife, for we all ought to join ourselves to some duty. Elsewhere, he who does not beget children on his wife is cursed:[73] he is wretched because he does not produce good and renowned works according to his duty. Having neglected their own wives, such people seek a different wife—such are those who choose another duty and did not commit themselves to the abandoned duty; and so adultery—inconstancy—occurs. Therefore, those struck down because of adultery are those who are rebuked for their inconstancy. *Arma:* we said that weapons allegorically are the powers of the soul; they are truly called pious because the enemy is struck down by them; vices are uprooted, their kin are defended, and virtues are preserved by them. This happens when irascibility fights vice, desire champions knowledge, and vehemence turns away vice and defends virtue. We say that these weapons are impious *(impia)* when their use is contrary—when irascibility enflames itself against virtue, concupiscence seeks vice, and animosity fights good and preserves vice or the wicked. *Dominorum:* just as we call the members of the body servants, so conversely we call the powers and judgments of the spirit masters—irascibility, desire, vehemence, wit, reason, memory. Therefore, those failing their pledges to their leaders *(Dextras dominorum)* are those who pervert the appropriate good acts of the spiritual powers: discovery by wit, discretion through reason, and tenacity of memory. Virgil therefore notes the seven classes of those living the wicked life: first, the envious, when he says "those who hated their brothers" *(quibus invisi fratres);* second, the arrogant: "he who had struck a parent" *(pulsatusve parens);* third, the negligent: "those who deceived a client" *(fraus, etc.);* fourth, the merciless: "those who set aside no share" *(nec partem)* of their gains; fifth, the inconstant: "for their adultery" *(quique ob adulterium);* sixth, the obstinate: "weapons" *(quique arma, etc.);* seventh, the weak. *Inclusi:* tangled wickedness.

[616–21] *Forma:* the kind of fate. *Fortuna:* the kind of life. *Saxum:* laborious endeavor. *Radiis rotarum:* the turns of Fortune. Fortune spins like a wheel setting some at the top, some at the bottom, pushing some from the top to the bottom, and raising some from the bottom to the top; whence one says:

Being raised up, I gloat; having descended, I am made less; being lowest, I am crushed by the axle; I will again be raised to the heights.

Therefore Fortune is figured forth by a wheel.[74] *Pendent:* the ones who "hang" are the doubters, as Macrobius explains *(Commentary* 1. 10. 4). *Teseus infelix:* wisdom beset by misery. The miseries of this life greatly oppress philosophers, as is clear (on the authority of Boethius) in the cases of Socrates, Seneca, Anaxagoras, Canius, and Soranus, whose wisdom was always attacked by the wicked *(Consolation,* bk. 1, prose 3. 9). *Flegias:* virtue, as if *flegeon,* that is, *ardens,* "burning," whence virtue elsewhere is called fiery.[75] Phlegyas is very miserable *(miser-*

rimus) because he must endure all labors. *Voce:* instruction. *Umbras:* temporal goods. *Discite:* behold the encouragement of virtue. *Divos:* knowledge and wisdom. *Vendidit:* here one must note the examples of virtue as well as of vice.

[625] *Non mihi:* it is sacrilege for the chaste to enter Tartarus, and therefore the Sibyl does not lead Aeneas there. By this we are informed that understanding does not place the contemplating spirit into the wicked life, lest it be defiled, but nevertheless understanding reveals the errors of the wicked to the spirit. And hence the Sibyl has told Aeneas what is in Tartarus. The Sibyl has a hundred mouths *(centum ora)* since understanding has a hundred utterances. *Formas:* kinds.

[629–30] *Viam:* contemplation. *Perfice:* since you know what is in Tartarus, it remains to inquire what is in Elysium. *Menia:* the visible having been traversed, it remains to examine the invisible carefully, and therefore the Sibyl tells Aeneas to look to the Heavens, namely the walls of the Cyclops. *Ciclops,* as if *policiculos,* that is, *multitudo circulorum,* "the multitude of circles." Circles, having no endpoint and centering on an indivisible and immutable point, figure immortal spirits cleaving to the indivisible and immutable Creator. A Cyclops, "the multitude of circles," is the order of spirits; many Cyclops are the multitudes of spirits. Therefore the walls of the Cyclops are the heavens, the natural regions of the spirits.[76] *Conspicio:* heavenly things lie open to understanding. *Educta:* higher than the others. *Caminis:* in the fiery houses which are the twelve parts of the sky. We read that not only is the zodiac divided into twelve parts by philosophers, but so too is the sky divided from the south pole to the arctic pole. Whence the southern and northern signs are said to be in no part of the zodiac or are said to be stars superior to it.

[631–36] *Atque fornice:* this is the vault of the human brain. *Portas:* the three chambers. We come to heavenly contemplation through these (as we said before) by exercising wit, reason, and memory. *Adverso:* Aeneas turns his head and looks to heaven. *Hec ubi:* at the gates, since Aeneas and the Sibyl are presently in the cells of memory.[77] *Dona:* philosophy. *Pariter:* because they enter together. *Viarum:* of virtues. *Medium:* that virtue which is the mean between human and divine substances. *Foribus propinquant:* "they approach the gates" when with wit they discover something, with reason they discern it, and they commit it to memory. *Occupat:* Aeneas occupies the entrance *(aditum)* when he exercises wit. *Corpus spargit recenti aqua:* "he sprinkles his body with fresh water" when he refreshes himself with new instruction. For the exercise of wit and the instruction of doctrine must be joined together, as Horace says: "If a praiseworthy song is to happen in nature or in art, it must be sought" *(Art of Poetry* 408–9). But since committing to memory follows discovery by wit, Aeneas places the branch *(ramum)*—philosophy—across the threshold *(adverso limine),* the rear chamber.

Here end the glosses on the *Aeneid*
according to the integument[78]

Notes

PREFACE

1. Bernardus may here be trying to distinguish the *Aeneid* from the *Eclogues* and the *Georgics* by its persistent use of fiction which conveys its philosophical content. According to Fulgentius, Virgil's earlier poems are "so bestrewn with mystical matters that in them Virgil has concealed the innermost profundities of almost every art" (*Fulgentius*, p. 119). The closest approximation to the quotation of Marcrobius is his *Commentary* 1. 9. 8; see also 2. 10. 11.

2. Landino in his commentary on the *Aeneid* in *The Camaldulensan Disputations* follows what Bernardus here describes as natural order, beginning his allegoresis with Aeneas's origins in Troy. Both Bernardus and Fulgentius follow the sequence of the *Aeneid*, starting their interpretations with the storm at sea, which both interpret as birth, and proceeding from there in the loose pattern of the ages of man.

3. The usual seven are (1) author's life, (2) title of the work, (3) poetic genre, (4) author's intention, (5) number of books, (6) order of the books, (7) explanation. (This is the list Servius uses in his commentary on the *Aeneid*). See E. R. Curtus, *European Literature and the Latin Middle Ages* (New York: Pantheon, 1953), p. 221; Edwin A. Quain, "The Medieval *Accessus ad Auctores*," *Traditio*, 2 (1944), 319–407; and R. B. C. Huygens, *Accessus ad Auctores; Bernard D'Utrecht; Conrad D'Hirsau: Dialogus super Auctores* (Leiden: E. J. Brill, 1970). Bernardus's three derive ultimately from such sources as Cicero *On Invention* 1. 15. 20.

4. *Commentary* 1. 9. 1–2; Juvenal *Satires* 11. 27. Bernardus garbles the Greek phrase "gnothi seauton." See also Macrobius *Saturnalia* 1. 6. 6.

BOOK I

1. So too Fulgentius. Landino, on the other hand, associates the first age with the sensual life before reason awakens and, in Virgil's poem, with Aeneas's Trojan origins.

2. Fulgentius gives the same etymology, similarly stresses Juno's role as the goddess of birth, and so also understands the storm and shipwreck as birth. Landino takes Juno as the goddess of riches and worldly ambition and consequently associates her with the active or civic life as opposed to the contemplative which, in his reading of the *Aeneid*, Virgil's hero ought to seek; the storm then represents the stirrings of appetite for worldly glory, which deflects Aeneas and his crew from their journey to Italy, which Landino identifies with contemplation.

3. Landino offers a similar list: *levis, mobilis, calidus, humidus, serenus, taciturnus, spirabilis*. His account of the attendants of Iris also resembles—and probably draws on—Bernardus's.

4. Landino reads Deiopeia similarly as the clarity of the heavens; Fulgentius etymologizes her name somewhat differently to arrive at "public vision" *(Fulgentius*, p. 125).

5. *Georgics* 3. 132; Virgil, however, advises this for the time of conception, not of birth. Bernardus was clearly no farmer.

6. Fulgentius etymologizes Anchises as "living in one's own land" *(Fulgentius*, p. 132) but understands the significance in the same way as Bernardus. At this point Fulgentius says nothing about Venus, although elsewhere (in *The Mythologies*) he rather consistently interprets her as concupiscence. Landino distinguishes two Venuses in Bernardus's manner and identifies the good one, Aeneas's mother, as the celestial love of Plato's *Symposium*. He interprets Anchises very differently, however, as the mortal half of Aeneas's ancestry and makeup and therefore identifies him with sense, sensation. or sensuality.

7. Bernardus here refers to Martianus Capella's lengthy allegory *The Marriage of Mercury and Philology*.

8. Bernardus more fully discusses the body as the prison of the soul in Book 6. Fulgentius does not give an etymology of Aeneas's name but does treat him throughout his commentary as equivalent to Everyman or Mansoul; Landino reads his name as derived from the Greek word for praise and regards him as an exceptional man destined to glory.

9. The commonplace may originate in Terence *The Eunuch* 732; Bernardus uses this frequently.

10. Throughout his commentary, Bernardus uses the Platonic prin-

ciple of the preexistent soul. His explanation of *Aeneid* 4 builds upon the kind of "psychological" commentary he offers here.

11. Fulgentius relates all this to the ignorance and aimlessness of infancy; Landino, to the allurements of the active life, for which Carthage is a figure. Bernardus quotes Boethius *Consolation*, bk. 3, prose 9. 30 and may also be referring to *Consolation*, bk. 3, prose 1. 5 and bk. 5, meter 4, 1. 12.

12. Cf. Apoc. 14:8 and Gen. 11:9. This trope becomes a commonplace of Christian homiletic literature, as in Augustine's *The City of God*.

13. Fulgentius's explanation of this is almost identical to Bernardus's.

14. Fulgentius: "Aeneas sees Cupid, for the way of an infant is always to covet *(cupere)* and desire something" *(Fulgentius*, p. 126).

BOOK 2

1. Bernardus cites Dares Phrygius's *The History of the Fall of Troy* (*De excidio Troiae historia*).

BOOK 3

1. Fulgentius: "In books 2 and 3, Aeneas is diverted by such tales as those by which a garrulous child is usually diverted" *(Fulgentius*, p. 126). That is Fulgentius's only comment on the events of books 2 and 3, except for his remarks on the Cyclops and the burial of Anchises, noted below.

2. The metaphor of the body as city is another commonplace; Bernardus will again use this trope in Book 6.

3. *Epistles* 1. 1. 98, 100. See also Jer. 1:10.

4. Bernardus is probably punning on *silva*, "grove," and *silva*, "matter" (in a philosophical sense); Bernardus's surname (Silvestris) is, of course, derived from *silva*. Landino also takes Ida as beauty, deriving it from the Greek word for form and interpreting it as the love of beauty that leads away from evil.

5. Horace *Epistles* 1. 6. 37–38. Landino quotes these same lines in his commentary on Aeneas's sojourn in Thrace, which he likewise interprets as avarice: in his view, Aeneas has now moved from the pleasure of sense to another kind of desire, equally far from the good.

6. All three quotations in this paragraph are from Horace: *Epistles* 1. 7. 71; *Epistles* 1. 1. 45; *Satires* 1. 1. 70–72.

7. The four quotations are Horace *Art of Poetry* 170; *Art of Poetry*

171 (slightly altered); Juvenal *Satires* 14. 139; and Horace *Epistles* 1. 2. 56.

8. Persius *Satires* 6. 68–70. As Bernardus's quotations from Horace, Persius, and Juvenal indicate, avarice provided one of the major targets of classical satire; Bernardus is clearly trying to place what he sees as Virgil's diatribe against the vice in that context, although in this case he appears to have missed Persius's irony.

9. Landino gives the same etymology and interpretation for Anius. He is also near to Bernardus on Delos: he takes it as *manifestum*—the clear and manifest place where wisdom reigns.

10. Landino's interpretation of the oracle is almost identical to Bernardus's.

11. Fulgentius's etymology is different, but the tenor of his reading is the same as Bernardus's: "Childhood . . . roams freely in its youthful wildness" *(Fulgentius,* p. 127). Landino, in accordance with his dialectic of civic and retired lives, reads the Cyclops as tyranny.

12. In *The Mythologies,* Fulgentius offers a similar etymology *(Fulgentius,* pp. 73–74).

13. Fulgentius gives the same etymology for Polyphemus and a very similar interpretation of the blinding.

14. Fulgentius has it as "boyish zest" rejecting parental discipline *(Fulgentius,* p. 127).

BOOK 4

1. *Art of Poetry* 161–62. Here as elsewhere, Bernardus is documenting the attributes of the age he claims Virgil allegorically depicts—in this case, by reference to Horace's descriptions of the character and actions appropriate to each.

2. Bernardus again refers to Martianus Capella's allegory *The Marriage of Mercury and Philology.*

3. Bernardus more fully discusses the relationship of wisdom and eloquence in Book 6.

4. Fulgentius's brief explanation of *Aeneid* 4 parallels the ethical portion of Bernardus's reading very closely, though none of Bernardus's physiology is present. Landino explains this book in a radically different manner: Carthage is the model republic, Dido the attractions of the civic life, which temporarily seduce the good man from his progress toward contemplation.

BOOK 5

1. Fulgentius considers these games as bodily exercise in deeds of valor, though he compares the boxing match to the discipline inflicted

by teachers *(Fulgentius,* pp. 127–28). Landino thinks the games only a lighter interlude introduced by Virgil for variety and respite from his serious discourse.

2. Landino similarly understands the episode as the rebellion of the inferior reason, stirred up by Juno (worldly greatness, ambition) against the superior. Fulgentius, on the other hand, reads it honorifically as the "fire of the intellect" consuming the reckless impulses of youth (Whitbread, p. 128).

3. *Timaeus* 35A, but probably transmitted through Calcidius's commentary.

4. Fulgentius gives the same etymology; Landino does not comment on Beroë.

5. Fulgentius and Landino give similar etymologies and explanations of Palinurus.

BOOK 6

1. Landino also refers at length to the Platonic notion of the body as the prison of the soul and brings it to bear upon Virgil's sixth book. Bernardus is probably drawing on Macrobius *Commentary* 1. 10–11.

2. Landino gives similar interpretations, though he adds Cocytus to the list of rivers and identifies Styx as a swamp.

3. Landino makes the same bipartite division. See also Macrobius *Commentary* 1. 10.

4. Landino lists five ways: Platonically, by birth; in the Christian view, as the final punishment for sin; morally, by vice; metaphorically, by necromancy and magic; intellectually, by contemplation of the nature of vice and evil. Aeneas, of course, is about to perform the last.

5. Bernardus's rather strained reading of the burial of Misenus as a magical rite may result from his prefatory assertion of Virgil's consistent use of both fiction and philosophy: the contemplative descent in the allegory needs to be balanced by a comprehensible event in the fiction.

6. Landino distinguishes between the temple of Apollo, the place of the divine, and the grove of Trivia, the wood of matter. Fulgentius understands the temple of Apollo as "studious learning"; after this, in order to consider his future life, Aeneas will "penetrate obscure and secret mysteries of knowledge" *(Fulgentius,* p. 128). Bernardus draws upon the common medieval division of the seven liberal arts into the trivium (grammar, dialetic, rhetoric) and the quadrivium (arithmetic, music, geometry, astronomy).

7. Fulgentius offers a very similar etymology but understands the significance of Achates's companioning Aeneas to lie in the hardships incumbent upon human life.

8. This definition derives from William of Conches's *Glosses on Calcidius's Preface;* see also Cicero *On Invention* 1. 25. 36.

9. So too Landino interprets the Sybil on the basis of a nearly identical etymology derived ultimately from the Greek for "divine counsel," *theou* or *siou boule.*

10. For the parts of eloquence, see Book 6, 1. 392.

11. Cf. Heb. 6:19: "This hope we have, as a sure firm anchor of the soul. . . ." But the image is ubiquitous.

12. Cf. Isa. 30:15: "For thus saith the Lord God the Holy One of Israel: 'If you return and be quiet, you shall be saved: in silence and in hope shall your strength be.'"

13. Fulgentius simply says that Aeneas is now done with "the shipwreck of unstable youth" *(Fulgentius,* p. 128). Landino glosses Aeneas's arrival in Italy as the soul's achievement of the stability of the purgative virtues; all its desires are now subject to the mind (Aeneas).

14. He refers once again to Martianus Capella's *The Marriage of Mercury and Philology* 8. 883.

15. Landino remarks that, although the soul, while it is exiled in the body, may devote itself completely to contemplation, it nevertheless cannot neglect the things that are necessary to the body: thus some seek fire, etc.

16. Allegedly in *The History of the Fall of Troy,* but Dares does not mention Aeneas coming to Deiphobe.

17. Landino similarly understands the flight of Daedalus as contemplation, though he takes the engraved fables as depictions of vices which Aeneas must briefly recognize.

18. Bernardus's etymology is a pun: *laborintus* (classical spelling *labyrinthus*), "labyrinth" = *labor intus,* "interior labor." And just as Theseus performs great labor within the maze of the labyrinth, so Aeneas must go through an analogous maze on his journey to wisdom.

19. Fulgentius gives similar explanations of the three Fates in *The Mythologies* 1. 8 *(Fulgentius,* p. 52). The quotation is from Hildebertus Cenomannensis *Carmina miscellanea* 138. 12.

20. *Consolation,* bk. 5, prose 4. 26–36. See also below, p. 53.

21. *Timaeus* 27C. Bernardus may also be citing Plato through Boethius *Consolation* bk 3, prose 9. 32.

22. See also Book 6, 1.495.

23. See Book 3 and *Aeneid* 3. 1–5.

24. Cf. *Aeneid* 9. 619.
25. Cf. *The Marriage of Mercury and Philology* 1. 27–28. Landino in his reading of this prayer emphasizes the hardness of the marble as indicative of the endurance of the mind devoted to wisdom.
26. *Theaetetus* 194C. This is also found in Calcidius's commentary on the *Timaeus* 328, a more likely source for Bernardus.
27. See. Prov. 5:16.
28. The anonymous medieval *Distichs of Cato* 2. 24.
29. Landino understands the Sibyl to be warning Aeneas of the dangers of renewed memory of and desire for the active life which will attack him in the solitude of the contemplative life.
30. Cf. 1 Cor. 13:12.
31. Ovid 2. 397; in Ovid, it is Jove who threatens.
32. This is a common medieval trope; for example, see Isa. 40:16, James 1:10, 1 Pet. 1:24; similarly, Eccles. 14:18.
33. This refers either to Paul's conversion (Acts 9:1–22) or to his being rapt to the third heaven (2 Cor. 12:2–4).
34. None of the manuscripts of the *Commentary* supplies the promised diagram. In their edition the Joneses give the following diagram, which they have adapted from a similar one in Bernardus Silvestris's *Commentary on Martianus Capella:*

Philosophy

Practical   Theoretical

Individual-Private-Public   Theology-Mathematics-Physics

35. Landino interprets the bough as wisdom, because it is golden; Fulgentius reads it as learning *(Fulgentius,* pp. 129–30). He also reads the Hesperides slightly differently as "study, intellect, memory, and eloquence" *(Fulgentius,* p. 129).
36. Both Fulgentius *(Fulgentius,* p. 128) and Landino offer similar overall interpretations of Misenus and his burial, differing only in details; Bernardus, however, is unique in the attention he will later pay to the details of Misenus's funeral pyre.
37. Cf. *Fulgentius,* p. 128.
38. *Consolation,* bk. 3, prose 1. 7 and probably also bk. 2 in general.
39. "Rhetoric" probably refers to rhetoric in general and more specifically to Cicero's *On Invention* 2. 53–54, 159–165.
40. Cf. Boethius *Consolation,* bk. 4, prose 3. 17–24; also, Bernardus's discussion of Circe in Book 3.

41. *Viscum* is usually read as "mistletoe," but Bernardus takes it, at least for purposes of his commentary, as "gum."

42. Eccles. 15:3; Job 28:25 and Isa. 40:12; Ps. 148:4; Prov. 9:17.

43. Fulgentius etymologizes Corynaeus as worldly favor *(Fulgentius,* p. 129).

44. Modern texts of Virgil read *viros* rather than *domos.*

45. The Joneses' edition has "ETERNUM . . ." after this sentence: there appears to be a lacuna.

46. Landino similarly refrains from commenting on Aeneas's sacrificing, simply noting that these were the magical rites of the ancients.

47. Fulgentius provides comparable explanations of the Furies, partially in his commentary on the *Aeneid (Fulgentius,* p. 131) and more fully in *The Mythologies (Fulgentius,* p. 32).

48. In the elaborate interpretation of the elm tree and its contents that now follows, Bernardus differs greatly from Landino's equally elaborate but more personalistic and psychological reading of the same Virgilian figure. Fulgentius does not comment on it at all in his treatment of Virgil, and there are many divergences between Bernardus's understanding of the various mythological figures and Fulgentius's explanations of them (frequently euhemeristic) in *The Mythologies.*

49. *Satires* 14. 129–30 (not quoted exactly).

50. Horace *Art of Poetry* 170. See also Polydorus in Book 3.

51. This seems to be an inexact quotation of Hildebertus Cenomannensis's translation (in his *Moralis philosophia)* of Euripides' *Andromeda* 319–20.

52. Bernardus reads *auras* for *umbras.*

53. *Consolation,* bk. 1, prose 4. 36 (not quoted exactly).

54. Fulgentius too translates Charon as time, though he takes *Polydegmon (sic)* as much knowledge *(Fulgentius,* p. 130). Landino, on the other hand, interprets Charon's boat as the will, Charon as the will's free choice, his pole as election, all moving Aeneas toward contemplation.

55. Cf. *Consolation,* bk. 1, meters 1 and 2.

56. *Timaeus* 45C and also 43A, B.

57. Cf. Macrobius *Commentary* 1. 13. 5; Plato *Phaedrus* 64A.

58. Juvenal *Satires* 10. 217–55, especially 253, 218–19, 227–29.

59. Fulgentius and Landino give the same etymology for Cerberus, but they interpret the figure differently: for Fulgentius, Cerberus represents the wrangling of lawyers *(Fulgentius,* p. 130), not quite eloquence, as Bernardus has it; for Landino, Cerberus is the earth and the insatiableness of the body.

60. Cf. Cicero *On Invention* 1. 1, and *On the Orator* 3. 15. Bernardus

Notes

refers directly to Martianus Capella *The Marriage of Mercury and Philology* 1. 24ff.

61. Cf. Ps. 18:11. Fulgentius interprets the sop in an identical manner *(Fulgentius*, p. 130); for Landino it represents the necessary and moderate care of the body.

62. Cf. *Aeneid* 4. 190.

63. Bernardus may be referring to "courtly love," now best known from Andreas Capellanus's *The Art of Courtly Love*.

64. Bernardus refers to Terence *The Eunuch* 65–66, 91–94, 152–54, 225–27, etc.

65. Terence *The Eunuch* 732. See discussion of Venus in Book 1 and of the Trojan horse in Book 6, 1. 515.

66. Fulgentius gives a similar interpretation of Deiphobus.

67. *Natural History* 8. 67. 166; cf. Virgil *Georgics* 3. 271–75.

68. Terence *The Eunuch* 732. See also note 65.

69. Fulgentius takes the walled city of Tartarus with its lofty walls as a symbol of sinful pride *(Fulgentius*, p. 131); for Landino, the triple walls represent the threefold nature of sin: conception, act, habit.

70. *Satires* 2.2. 77–79 (not quoted exactly).

71. These epithets are commonplaces; Bernardus may well have drawn them from Virgil *Eclogues* 3. 60 and Macrobius *Commentary* 1. 17. 14.

72. Horace *Satires* 1. 2. 5–6 (not quoted exactly).

73. Perhaps referring to Gen. 38:8–10 or Ruth 4:10.

74. This description of Fortune and her wheel is a medieval commonplace. Cf. *Consolation*, bk. 2, meter 1. See also H. R. Patch, *The Goddess Fortuna in Medieval Literature* (Cambridge, Mass.: Harvard University Press, 1924).

75. For example, Lucan *Pharsalia* 9. 7; see also Book 6, 1. 130.

76. Fulgentius takes the Elysian fields as the life of the mature man, now arrived at true knowledge and freed from his teachers *(Fulgentius*, pp. 131–32). Landino takes the fields as a figure of heaven, the reward for successful contemplatives like Orpheus and Musaeus, as well as for some pious statesmen. Aside from a brief discussion of the Platonic cosmology that the shade of Anchises imparts to Aeneas, this is effectively the terminal point of Landino's exposition.

77. Similarly Fulgentius: Aeneas "celebrates the perfecting of memory, which is to be fastened in the brain as enduringly as the golden bough on the gateposts" *(Fulgentius*, p. 132).

78. This *explicit* appears in only one manuscript. The commentary that can be reasonably ascribed to "Bernardus" breaks off at this point, and the continuation published by the Joneses in their edition

is clearly not by the same hand, as the Joneses have argued in their introduction. Landino's commentary, as noted in our introduction and above, n. 76, also effectively ends at this point with the achievement of contemplation; Fulgentius goes on to comment briefly about the remaining six books of the *Aeneid*, primarily in terms of Aeneas's meeting and overcoming various vices and dangers and culminating in his victory over Turnus and Juturna, who represent rage and destruction.

Index

This index omits references to Aeneas (because he appears throughout the *Commentary*), to the Translators' Introduction, and to the notes.

Abisides, 7
Abstinence, 41
Achaemenides, 17, 22; etymology of, 24
Achates, 33, 39; etymology of, 34
Acheron, 32, 51, 67, 76–78, 82, 84, 85, 86; etymology of, 76
Achilles, etymology of, 45–46
Active life, 47, 85
Adolescence, 17, 18, 22, 24, 43
Adrastus, 91–92
Adultery, 25, 26, 96, 104, 105
Aeacus, etymology of, 87–88
Aello, etymology of, 71
Aeneid, 3–4, 107
Aeolus, 6, 10, 12; etymology of, 7
Aesculapius, 37
Aetna, 22–24
Affection, 41
Africa, 83
Afroden, 26
Agamemnon, etymology of, 92
Age, 6, 14–16, 18, 26, 32, 40, 43, 48, 49, 52, 63, 79, 82, 84, 85, 91, 94
Aglaia, 57
Air, 6, 7–9, 10, 36, 47, 52, 64, 65, 67, 100
Alcides, 19, 55–56, etymology of, 82–83
Alecto, 67

Allegory, 5, 11, 16, 17, 25, 32, 33, 37, 39, 41, 45, 46, 48, 51, 57, 69, 72, 101, 104
Aloeus, etymology of, 101
Aloides, 101, 102, 104
Altar, 58
Alteration, 43
Ambiguities, 51, 69
Anaxagoras, 105
Anchises, 4, 11, 12, 29, 52–53; etymology of, 10
Anchor, 35
Andreas, etymology of, 18
Androgeus, 39
Angels, 29, 42, 52, 62
Anger, 23, 24, 37, 103, 104
Animals, 26, 29, 31–32, 37, 40, 52, 61, 65, 68, 74, 96, 97. *See also* Beasts *and names of individual animals*
Anius, etymology of, 20–21
Antandros, 17, 19; etymology of, 18
Antarctic, 78
Antenorides, 92
Antilochus, 46, 82
Anxiety, 20, 97, 99, 103
Aplanen, 32
Aplanes, 48
Apollo, 11, 20, 21, 36–38, 45–46, 53–54, 56, 79, 103
Apostates, 24

119

Index

Appetite, 4, 14, 15, 54, 55, 59
Apple. *See* Golden apple
Arctic, 79
Arethusa, 57
Ariopagus, etymology of, 54
Aristaeus, etymology of, 53–54
Arms, 24, 62, 67, 82, 94, 95, 98, 102, 104–5
Army, 46, 91, 92, 94
Arrows, 28, 46, 71
Arteries, 12, 26
Artifice, 33, 57
Artificial order, 3–4
Arts, 33–35, 37–41, 45, 85, 86, 97, 107
Ascanius, 4, 6; etymology of, 14–15
Ascent, 45, 52, 76
Ash (tree), 61
Asia, 83
Astrea, 11
Athens, 39
Atropos, 43
Augustus, 3
Aurora, 7
Ausonia, 80
Authors, 39, 40. *See also* Poet
Autumn, 76
Avarice, 19–21, 37, 61, 72, 96–97, 104. *See also* Greed
Avernus, 53

Babbling, 14
Babylon, 14
Bacchus, 12, 48, 65, 91, 96, 97
Banquet, 6, 14, 21
Battle, 59, 76, 77, 102
Beasts, 23, 31, 37, 61, 68–69
Beatitude, 21
Beauty, 19, 44, 56, 58, 63, 65–67, 78, 83, 90
Bible, quotations from: *1 Corinthians*, 52; *Ecclesiasticus*, 64; *Isaiah*, 64–65; *Job*, 64; *Michaea*, 62; *Philippians*, 61; *Psalms*, 62, 65; *Proverbs*, 49, 65
Birds, 26, 62, 71, 76
Birth, 7, 10, 12, 32, 43, 51, 54, 57, 64, 67, 72, 92, 94
Bitterness, 20, 29, 61, 101

Blindness, 22, 60, 71, 80, 84, 94
Blood, 70
Boat, 74, 84, 85. *See also* Fleet; Ship
Body, 5, 9–14, 17–19, 21, 24, 26, 29, 35, 36, 40–43, 46, 52, 55, 56, 62, 63, 65–68, 72, 74–76, 82–85, 89–95, 97, 101, 104, 105
Boethius, 13, 21, 23, 29, 31, 35, 38, 42, 44, 50, 51, 53, 60, 61, 69, 73, 74, 78, 82, 87, 89, 105
Boldness, 62, 78
Bones, 77, 83
Books, 14, 33, 37
Boreas, 71, 72
Bough, 58–60
Boxing, 28
Brain, 12, 26, 47, 106
Branch, 42, 57–59, 63, 67, 84, 107
Briareus, 68–69
Brother, 55, 70, 84, 93, 105
Bull, 39
Bullocks, 40, 41
Burial, 17, 19, 20, 24, 25, 59, 64–66, 75, 77, 78, 95

Caeneus (Caenis), 89–90
Calais, etymology of, 71–72
Calliope, 37, 56; etymology of, 53–54
Cancer, 7, 65
Canius, 105
Capaneus, 89
Carthage, 6, 13–14
Caspian Sea, 78
Cassandra, 37
Castor, 55
Cave, 25, 26, 38, 41, 42, 51, 85
Celaeno, etymology of, 71
Cells, 12
Censure, 27, 93
Centaurs, 68
Cerberus, 82, 84–86; etymology of, 83
Ceres, 12, 48, 91, 96; etymology of, 58
Chain, 11, 39, 81–83
Chaldeans, 83
Chambers, 47, 68, 107
Charon, 74–76, 82, 84–85; etymology of, 73

Index

Chastity, 41
Childbirth, 7, 12
Childhood, 18; etymology of, 16
Children, 6, 12, 16, 18, 37, 56, 75, 104
Chimaera, 69, 89
Cicero, 83
Circe, 37; etymology of, 22–23
Circle, 22, 23, 73, 84, 106
Circumlocution, 84
Citadel, 17, 97, 102
City, 13, 14, 16–19, 34, 35, 45, 46, 74, 93–97, 99, 101, 102, 104
Cliff, 99
Clio, 37
Clotho, 43
Cloud, 6, 8, 9, 13, 14, 68, 78, 102
Cocytus, 57, 73, 77, 78, 81
Cohabitation, 87, 88
Coldness, 7, 8, 10, 48, 49, 57, 58, 63, 65, 74, 76, 83, 104
Comet, 9
Companions, 6, 12, 14, 19, 23, 24, 36, 37, 39, 48, 55, 62, 78, 79, 104
Composition, 4
Concord, 11, 12, 41, 63
Concupiscence, 11, 54, 62, 78
Confusion, 13, 14
Conscience, 65–70, 89, 99, 103
Constancy, 18
Constellations, 7, 65
Contemplation, 42, 47, 52, 60, 62, 63, 65, 66, 77–79, 81–84, 90–92, 98, 99, 106
Copulation, 11, 69
Corinna, etymology of, 66
Coronides, etymology of, 66
Corporeality, 21, 42
Corruption, 43
Coryneus, etymology of, 66
Counsel, 22, 25, 34, 41, 43, 76, 80
Cowardice, 61
Creator, 11, 25, 29, 30, 32, 42, 46, 51, 52, 62, 80, 82, 84, 87, 91, 102, 106
Crete, 4, 17, 100; etymology of, 21
Creusa, etymology of, 14
Crown, 48
Crying, 87

Cumaea, etymology of, 34–35
Cupid, 6, 11, 14
Cupidity, 101
Cybele, etymology of, 47–48
Cyclops, 17; etymology of, 22, 106
Cymothoë, etymology of, 13
Cypress, 64

Daedalus, 38–39
Dares Phrygius, 3, 16, 37, 45–46
Darkness, 99
Daughter, 7, 22, 23, 46, 58, 67, 69, 70, 75, 84, 90
Day, 12, 66, 70, 74, 75, 94, 101
Death, 43, 54, 55, 62, 75, 76, 78, 88–91, 95
Defense, 91, 93
Deficiency, 15
Deiopea, 6, 7, 12; etymology of, 10
Deiphobe, 37, 38
Deiphobus, 79, 93, 98; etymology of, 95
Deities, 48. *See also* God *and* Goddess *and names of individual deities*
Delius, 20, 38
Delos, 17; etymology of, 20
Demigod, 56, 82, 83
Demons, 83
Descent, 21, 28, 29, 31–33, 52, 53, 55–59, 65–66, 79, 82–84, 95, 98
Desire(s), 12–16, 18, 19, 23, 25, 28–30, 32–35, 37, 44, 45, 49, 50, 55, 56, 60, 62, 65, 70, 79, 87, 93, 96, 101, 104, 105
Dialectic, 33, 83, 85–87. *See also* Rhetoric
Dido, 4, 6, 13, 16, 25–28, 39, 79, 90–91
Digestion, 25, 68
Diogenes, 64, 88
Diomedes, 96
Dionysius, 103
Dis, 51, 66, 99–100
Disciplines, 42, 44, 104. *See also* Teaching
Discretion, 25, 38, 62, 71
Divination, 45. *See also* Future

Divinity, 7, 21, 22, 32, 34, 38, 41–43, 45, 49, 51, 53, 55, 64, 66, 67, 76, 78, 81, 83, 88, 101, 106
Doctrine, 49, 66, 79, 87, 107. *See also* Instruction *and* Teaching
Doris, etymology of, 20
Doves, 63; etymology of, 62
Dreams, 67–68
Drepanum, 17; etymology of, 24
Drink, 12, 25, 36, 41, 51, 65, 66, 89, 101
Drunkenness, 65, 91, 96, 97
Dryness, 10
Dwellings, 17–18, 46, 56, 61

Ear, 34, 72, 93, 94
Earth, 6, 7, 9, 10, 23, 38, 40, 41, 46–48, 51, 56–58, 63, 65–68, 70, 72, 74–76, 81, 83, 85, 97, 101, 103
Earthquake, 9
Eden, 32
Education. *See* Disciplines; Doctrine; Instruction; Teaching
Elements, 11, 36, 47, 65, 67, 74, 102
Elis, 102
Elm, 67
Eloquence, 11, 26, 33, 34, 36–38, 40, 48, 54–55, 70, 83–88, 95, 100, 103, 104
Elysium, 106; etymology of, 99
Enigmas, 50
Ennosigeum, 11
Equivocation, 11
Epicureans, 47, 72, 75, 79, 80, 91
Erato, 37
Erebus, 6, 58
Eriphyle, 89
Error, 42, 52, 54, 79–81, 85, 90–92, 99, 104, 106
Eternal, The, 24
Euboea, etymology of, 34
Euboean rocks, 41–42
Eumenides, 67
Europe, 83
Euryale, 69–70
Eurydice, 33, 53–55
Euterpe, 89

Evadne, 89
Evander, etymology of, 18
Evil, 22, 28, 37, 54, 62, 70, 74, 78, 81, 86–89, 91, 93–95, 101, 103, 104
Excess, 15
Exile, 3
Extremities, 94
Eye, 10, 13, 17, 24, 40, 46, 68–71, 75, 78, 79, 82, 91–94, 98, 99

Fables, 16, 20, 26, 38–39, 68
Face, 44, 55, 91
Fall, 74
Falseness, 13, 16, 51, 63, 87
Fame, 23, 24, 65, 70
Fantasies, 66
Farmers, 18, 102
Fate(s), 43, 91, 98, 105
Father, 6, 10, 24, 28–30, 56, 72, 75, 76, 79, 82, 104
Fear, 70, 86–87, 93–95, 97–101, 103, 104
Feet, 18, 40, 93, 94
Femininity, 89–90
Fiction, 33, 36, 51, 87
Fig (tree), 64
Figure, 4, 87, 96, 103
Fire, 6, 8–11, 36, 47, 48, 52, 56, 58, 64, 65, 67–69, 84, 90, 101, 103, 105, 106
Firmament, 73–74
First age, 6, 14, 15, 18, 48, 49, 79
Flame, 23, 36, 58, 65, 66, 82, 97, 103
Fleet, 23, 30, 33, 78
Flesh, 7, 11, 13, 21, 22, 25, 29, 32, 35, 40, 46, 48, 50, 52, 58–60, 64, 67, 70, 73, 75, 77, 84, 85, 97, 98, 101, 104
Food, 12, 14, 25, 41, 68, 71, 75, 76, 82, 89
Footrace, 28
Forgetfulness, 51
Forgiveness, 52
Fornication, 11, 96
Fortitude, 28
Fortune, 50, 60, 64, 77, 99, 102, 103, 105
Fosforos, 36

Index

Fraud, 61, 99
Friendship, 29, 41
Fulgentius, 59, 83
Future, 33, 38, 45, 49, 50, 51

Games, 28, 29
Ganymede, etymology of, 19
Generation, 43
Genitals, 12, 26, 40
Genius, 54
Gentleness, 41
Geryon, etymology of, 72
Giants, 101, 104; etymology of, 76
Gigantomachia, 76
Glaucus, 37, 92
Glory, 54, 56, 59–60, 62, 65, 66, 69, 70, 72, 82–83, 98, 99, 104
Glosses, 107
Gluttony, 26, 67, 78–79, 91, 96
God, 4, 6, 7, 11–13, 21, 24, 26, 28–30, 45, 49, 54–56, 59, 69, 71, 76–78, 80, 83, 84, 95, 100. *See also* Demigod *and names of individual gods*
Goddess, 6, 7, 11, 13, 20, 43, 46, 53, 58, 78, 93. *See also names of individual goddesses*
Golden apple, 47
Golden bough, 57, 58, 59
Golden leaf, 64
Golden roofs, 33, 39, 40
Good(s), 13, 14, 20–22, 28, 29, 38, 45, 47, 53–56, 60, 62, 70, 72, 77, 78, 81, 83, 86–89, 91, 93–95, 99, 101, 104, 105
Gorgons, etymology of, 69–70
Grammar, 33, 34, 83, 86, 87.
Grave, 24, 64, 75, 78. *See also* Burial
Greece, 46
Greed, 71, 89, 101. *See also* Avarice
Greek (language), 40
Greeks, 45–46, 79, 92–93, 95–96, 97
Grove, 19, 33, 34, 38–40, 53, 89
Growth, 21, 29, 46, 47, 68, 80
Gum, 63

Habit, 14, 23, 34, 51, 56, 71, 73, 81
Hail, 8, 74

Hands, 18, 23, 37, 40, 46, 72, 93, 94
Happiness, 13
Harlotry, 96
Harmony, 11, 29, 62
Harpies, 22, 70, 72; etymology of, 71
Hatred, 51, 66, 77, 88, 104
Head, 12, 40, 54, 63, 69, 71, 83, 98
Heat, 7–10, 12, 18, 23, 27, 29, 36, 48, 49, 58, 65, 67, 68, 74, 76, 83, 97, 103
Heart, 49, 98
Heaven(s), 10, 30, 44, 49, 55, 56, 60, 61, 63, 65, 102, 106
Hebrews, 74
Hecate, 53
Hector, 45–46, 60
Hecuba, 46
Helen, 97–98; etymology of, 93–94
Herbs, 23
Hercules, 32, 71–72; etymology of, 69, 82–83
Hermes, etymology of, 26. *See also* Mercury.
Herophile, 37
Hesper, 35–36
Hespera, 57
Hesperian shore, 36, 39
Histeron proteron, 52
History, 16, 37
Historians, 4, 72
Homer, 3
Honest life, 20
Honesty, 16
Hope, 35, 86–87, 100
Horace, 4, 18–20, 24–27, 54, 60, 72, 79, 80, 82, 87, 101, 103, 107
Horse, 28, 68, 70, 95–98
Horserace, 28
Humanity, 57, 63
Humors, 7, 9, 25, 36, 49, 65, 68, 74
Hunting, 25
Husband, 53, 58, 91
Hydra, 69, 100

Ida, 92; etymology of, 18–19
Idea, 45, 51, 53, 64, 67, 70, 81, 100
Ideus, 19, 92
Idleness, 96–97

Ignorance, 13, 38, 56, 61, 62, 66–69, 79, 80, 86, 89, 91, 94, 95, 99, 100, 102
Ilex, 61
Iliad, 3
Illusions, 89
Images, 13, 29, 58, 91
Imagination, 44, 66, 79, 89, 90
Imitation, 4, 72
Immortality, 21, 55
Incest, 89, 96
Inconstancy, 18, 19, 96–97, 104, 105
Incorporeals, 42
Indolence, 13
Inertia, 96–97
Infancy, 12–15, 43, 87; etymology of, 16
Infernal regions, 31–32. *See also* Underworld
Infernum, 32
Ingestion and elimination, 12
Innocence, 41
Inspiration, 49
Instability, 49, 62
Instruction, 4, 16, 28, 33, 38–40, 49, 58–59, 61, 63, 64, 66, 70, 71, 79, 80, 85, 86, 90, 91, 94, 95, 103, 106, 107. *See also* Teaching
Integrity, 83
Integument, 5, 107
Intellect, 39, 48, 59, 60, 69, 71
Intelligence, 49, 51–53
Interpretation, 10–12, 17, 20–22, 25, 26, 31, 33, 46, 50, 51, 53, 55, 57, 59, 61, 64–67, 69, 70, 75, 92, 98, 102, 104
Involucrum, 5
Iopas, 6; etymology of, 14
Irascibility, 62, 78, 105
Ire, 7, 51
Iris, 7, 8, 29
Irresponsibility, 96–97
Island, 22; etymology of, 23
Italy, 29, 46, 47, 48, 80; etymology of, 21
Ixion, etymology of, 68, 103

Jealousy, 89
Jocus, 11
Journey, 82
Jove, 6, 11, 67, 84, 87, 101, 102; etymology of, 56
Joy, 13, 24, 46, 73, 82, 86–87, 91, 100
Judge, 87, 103
Judgment, 21, 44, 62, 87, 98, 103, 105
Juno, 6, 8–10, 46–47, 58; etymology of, 7, 68
Jupiter, 6, 11, 56, 58, 66, 101–2
Justice, 11, 28, 29
Juvenal, 9, 11, 71, 72, 82, 91, 101, 103

King, 7, 9, 19, 21, 51, 58, 72, 82, 103
Knowledge, 5, 21, 22, 30, 34, 35, 37, 40–42, 45–47, 51–53, 56–58, 61, 62, 64–67, 69, 73, 75–83, 85, 87–90, 96, 98, 100, 101, 104–6

Labor, 4, 14, 23, 28, 35, 39, 41, 46, 47, 49, 50, 59, 60, 62, 64, 66, 77, 97, 101, 106
Lachesis, 43
Lake, 51
Lamentation, 57, 59, 65, 66, 89
Language, 10, 11, 23, 40
Laodamia, 89
Laomedon, 45
Lapithae, etymology of, 104
Latin, 40
Latium, 47
Latona, etymology of, 102–3
Laughter, 13
Law, 24, 41, 56, 88
Laziness, 7, 96–97
Leaf, 49, 63, 64, 67, 76
Learning, 12, 21, 37, 39, 42–44, 66, 87, 88. *See also* Instruction *and* Teaching
Lechery, 22, 36, 39, 61, 75, 80, 81, 88–91, 96, 97
Leftness, 13, 58, 99
Leo, 65
Lethe, 32, 51
Leucaspis, etymology of, 78

Index

Leucothoe, etymology of, 78
Liber, Bowl of Father, 65
Libya, 4
Life, 5
Light, 12, 13, 36, 40, 67, 73, 75, 80
Lightning, 9, 102
Logic, 40
Loins, 62
Love, 46, 54, 56, 59, 64, 83, 88–90, 101
Lucan, 4, 9, 56
Lucifer, etymology of, 36
Lucina, etymology of, 7
Lust, 7, 11, 12, 28

Macrobius, 3, 5, 38, 51, 65, 105
Madness, 7
Magic, 33, 57, 66
Malice, 51
Manhood, 25, 28, 43, 49, 89–90
Manliness, 18, 27
Mare, 10, 96
Marmensus, 37
Marriage, 26
Mars, 7, 77
Martianus Capella, 11, 35, 48, 83
Mathematical arts, 33–34
Mathematics, 18, 33, 37, 42, 44
Mean, the, 14–15
Mechanics, 34–38
Medicine, 37
Meditation, 32, 39
Medon, 92
Medusa, 57; etymology of, 69–70
Megaera, 67, 103
Melancholy, 10, 24, 36, 48
Melpomene, 37
Members, 40, 65, 66, 68
Memory, 12, 18, 37, 47, 48, 57, 58, 63, 75, 77, 78, 81, 90–91, 103, 105–7
Menelaus, 93–94, 98; etymology of, 92
Merchants, 26, 84, 102
Mercury, 11, 22, 23, 25, 27, 70, 83; etymology of, 26, 84
Metaphor, 12
Microcosmus, 102

Mind, 22, 25, 26, 32, 40, 43, 49–51, 59, 60, 63, 64, 66, 69, 72–74, 76, 77, 81, 83, 97, 98, 100, 103, 104
Minerva, 48; etymology of, 47
Minos, 38, 88; etymology of, 87
Misenus, 33, 62, 66, 75; etymology of, 59
Moderation, 28, 41
Modesty, 41
Moisture, 7, 8, 10, 50, 57, 58, 65, 68, 74, 85
Money, 19, 20, 27, 71
Monster, 68, 69, 72
Moon, 21, 36, 53, 58, 74, 84, 90
Mother, 11, 14, 21, 48, 62, 75, 103
Mountain, 23, 62, 66, 69, 81
Mourning, 62, 74–76, 78, 87, 99
Mouth, 49, 60, 83, 100
Multivocation, 11
Munificence, 61
Muses, 37, 98, 101

Narration, 3–4, 16, 45
Narrative, 5, 17, 25, 31, 33, 34, 47, 48, 62, 104
Natural Order, 3–4, 5
Necessity, 81, 92
Negligence, 7, 50
Neoptolemus, etymology of, 21
Neptune, 6, 45; etymology of, 11
Nestor, 46
Night, 67, 75, 94, 101
Noise, 14
Number, 18, 42, 71

Oak, 61, 64
Oblivion, 24, 32, 59, 60, 66, 76, 77, 81, 82, 88, 95
Obstinancy, 61
Ocean, 12
Ochiroe, etymology of, 71
Odyssey, 3
Old: age, 32, 43, 49, 63, 82, 84–85, 94; person, 18, 49, 84, 85, 94
Olympus, 101
Ops, 6

Oracle, 4, 21
Orcus, 83
Orgies, 97
Orontes, etymology of, 78
Orpheus, 32, 53, 55; etymology of, 54
Ovid, 8, 71, 89, 101
Pales, 48
Palinurus, 28, 33, 34, 75, 79–81; etymology of, 29–30
Pallas, 46–47, 70
Paradisus, 32
Parents, 75, 105
Paris, 45, 47, 92; etymology of, 46, 93
Parthenopaeus, 91
Pasiphaë, 38, 89
Passion, 7, 13, 18, 25, 27, 29, 35, 36, 39, 41, 46, 50, 52, 57, 60, 61, 64, 69, 79, 80, 84, 85, 90, 94, 96, 97
Patience, 4
Paul, 56
Peace, 66
Pegasus, 70, 98
Peleus, 82
Penance, 69, 89, 99
Peripatetics, 42
Pergama, 97
Perseus, 69–70
Perseverance, 37
Persius, 64
Phaedra, 89
Phaedria, 90
Philology, 26, 83
Philosophers, 3, 44, 47, 51, 62, 69, 74, 75, 88, 93, 102, 105
Philosophical: arts, 35, 38, 41–42; life, 85
Philosophize, to, 60, 64, 84, 95, 103
Philosophy, 3, 5, 7, 31, 33–42, 44, 49, 57–59, 61, 63, 64, 66, 67, 75, 79, 85, 88, 95, 106, 107. *See also* Theory; Practice
Phineus, etymology of, 71
Phlegethon, 32, 51, 99
Phlegyas, etymology of, 105
Phoebus, 7, 21, 36, 45, 46, 48, 49
Phorcys, etymology of, 70
Phrygian women, 97

Physics, 37, 42
Pictures, 13, 38, 40
Piety, 4, 37, 41
Pine trees, 61
Pirithous, 83–84
Planet, 101–2
Plato, 29, 45, 48, 49, 51, 68, 72, 75, 91, 92, 102
Platonists, 42
Playwrights, 4
Pleasure, 4, 11, 14, 22, 23, 32, 47, 50, 67, 72, 73, 75, 78–80, 85, 88, 95
Pliny, 96
Pluto, 6, 58, 84
Poet, 3, 4, 38, 39, 44, 72. *See also* Authors
Poetic: fiction, 3, 11, 16, 36, 51, 65, 69, 75, 83, 96, 102; study, 39, 40
Poetics, 34, 36, 37
Poetry, 36, 39, 40, 42, 72, 83
Poliboeten, 92
Politicians, 47
Polixena, 46
Pollux, 55
Polydaemon, 73–74
Polydorus, 19; etymology of, 20
Polyhymnia, 37, 48
Polymnestor, 20; etymology of, 19
Polyphemus, 17, 22; etymology of, 23
Potions, 23
Power(s), 17–19, 26, 29, 46, 50, 53, 60, 62, 65, 67, 80, 97–99, 102, 104, 105
Practice, 38, 42, 57, 63, 64, 70, 81, 83, 88, 103. *See also* Theory
Prayer, 4, 45, 48, 53, 56
Priam, 37; etymology of, 93–94
Pride, 23–24, 59–62, 100
Priest, 21
Priestess, 40, 41
Prince, 92
Prison, 12, 32
Procris, 89
Prodigality, 61, 96–97
Prophecy, 50–51
Prophetess, 49
Proportion, 11
Prose, 35

Index

Proserpina, 84; etymology of, 58
Prudence, 28, 94
Pythagoras, 57–58, 63
Pythagoreans, 42

Quadrivium, 40
Queen, 58
Quiet life, 76, 77, 85, 86

Race, 28
Rain, 8, 25, 26, 74
Rainbow, 8
Rashness, 61
Rationality, 21, 23
Reason, 12, 17, 28, 29, 33, 34, 39, 43–47, 53, 57, 59, 60, 62, 63, 66, 72, 73, 78, 84, 90–93, 103–7
Rebuke, 61, 71, 80–83, 85, 90, 100, 104
Recollection, 51
Religion, 41
Republic, 92, 102
Rhadamanthus, etymology of, 87–88
Rhetoric, 33, 40, 44, 54–55, 60, 64, 83, 85–87
Rhoeteum, etymology of, 95
Riches, 19, 51, 93
Rightness, 13, 58, 99
River, 32, 51, 53, 57, 73, 74, 77, 88
Robbery, 26, 71
Rock, 36, 41–42, 54
Romans, 37

Sacrifice, 4, 28, 40–42, 45, 46, 56, 66
Sadness, 46, 65, 73–79
Sagittarius, 74
Sailors, 50
Sallust, 51
Salmoneus, 104; etymology of, 102
Satirists, 4, 72
Saturn, 6, 7, 12, 48, 75, 102
Science(s), 33, 38, 103
Scylla, 68
Sea, 7, 12, 13, 20, 35, 45, 50, 59, 65, 69, 70, 78, 80
Seals, 50
Seasons, 11, 74–76, 94

Seawater, 20
Second age, 16
Secret, 38, 48, 51, 59, 65
Self-knowledge, 5
Seneca, 105
Sense, 13, 26, 29, 40, 44, 45–47, 54, 63, 67, 68, 75, 85, 93, 94, 98
September, 71
Serpent, 26, 54, 58, 69
Severity, 44
Shade, 55, 79, 90, 102
Shame, 41
Sheep, 40, 41, 69
Shepherd, 54
Ship, 6, 12–13, 18–19, 28, 29, 33–35, 50, 85, 93. *See also* Boat; Fleet
Shipwreck, 22, 50
Sibyl, 33, 35, 37–43, 45, 48–53, 57, 59, 66, 74, 82, 84–86, 99, 106; etymology of, 34
Sicheus, 91
Sicily, 4
Sigeum, 11
Sight, 62, 68, 69, 94
Significations, 11
Simplicity, 41
Sirius, etymology of, 65
Sister, 6, 67, 70, 100
Sleep, 67
Sloth, 96–97
Smoke, 9, 10
Snow, 8, 74
Sobriety, 41
Society, 29
Socrates, 102, 105
Sol Delius, 20
Soldiers, 102
Solomon, 49
Son, 10–12, 14, 15, 46, 53, 54, 71, 73, 75, 87, 90, 93, 101
Soranus, 105
Sorcerers, 57
Sorcery, 33
Sorrow, 32, 51, 57, 67, 73, 86–88, 100
Soul, 14, 23, 32, 37, 39, 41, 44, 46–48, 50–53, 55, 56, 60, 62–66, 75, 78, 80, 82, 84, 85, 91, 100–102, 104

Sparingness, 41
Sparks, 36
Speech, 4, 16, 26, 27, 33, 38, 40, 44, 54–55, 64, 67, 70, 82, 84, 86, 87, 99, 100, 103
Speechlessness, 14
Spirit, 5, 7, 11, 12, 15, 17–22, 28, 29, 31, 33–36, 40, 45, 49–51, 55, 56, 65–67, 75, 76, 79, 81–88, 90, 94, 95, 98–103, 106
Spring, 74, 75
Star, 9, 11, 26, 35, 36, 39, 55, 65, 79, 84
Statius, 70, 72
Stench, 61, 63, 68
Sthenno, 69–70
Stoics, 42, 75
Stomach, 25
Storm, 7–10, 22, 25, 50, 74, 78
Strength, 12, 56, 72, 83, 89, 91
Strophades, 17; etymology of, 22
Student, 59, 64, 75
Study, 12, 33–37, 39, 40, 42, 44, 49, 57, 59, 60, 63, 64, 69, 84, 97, 103
Styx, 32, 51, 76–77, 88
Summer, 74, 75, 94
Sun, 7–9, 11, 23, 29, 36, 53, 65, 68, 74, 84, 94, 95, 98–99, 101
Sunrise, 98–99
Sword, 70, 72, 82, 98
Syrtes, 46

Tartarus, 99–101, 106
Taurus, 39
Teacher, 49, 59, 63, 64, 75, 76, 78–80, 86, 104
Teaching, 3, 42, 45, 49, 51, 52, 66, 86–88, 90. *See also* Instruction
Temerity, 7
Temperance, 28, 49
Temple, 36, 38–41, 46, 48
Temporal, the, 24
Temporal: good(s), 13, 23, 36, 53–58, 60–63, 66, 68, 93, 95, 98–101, 104, 106; life, 21, 50, 66; matters, 53, 55; things, 35, 39, 57, 60
Terence, 4, 9

Terpsichore, 37
Terror, 70, 79
Tersilochus, 92
Teucer, etymology of, 94
Thais, 90
Thalia, 37
Theft, 23
Theodoric, 73
Theology, 21, 31, 37, 44, 51, 101
Theory, 37–39, 42, 57, 83, 88, 103. *See also* Practice
Theseus, 84; etymology of, 55, 83
Thought, 27, 29, 32, 33, 37, 40, 45, 47, 52, 55, 64, 65, 67, 68, 84, 100, 103
Thrace, 17, 19, 20, 55
Thunder, 9, 102
Timaeus. *See* Plato
Time, 6, 11, 61, 73–77, 82, 90, 96
Tisiphone, 67, 100
Titan, 76, 101
Tityus, 104; etymology of, 102–3
Torpor, 7
Torso, 40
Tower, 100
Tree, 52, 57, 58, 60–63, 67. *See also* individual names
Triton, 59; etymology of, 13
Trivia, 38, 40, 48; etymology of, 33
Trivium, 3, 33, 40
Trojan: horse, 95–96; women, 29, 97
Trojans, 3, 4, 41, 46, 94–97
Troy, 3, 4, 16, 17–19, 46, 47, 92–98
Truculence, 61
Trumpet, 13, 59, 84, 102
Truth, 3, 13, 5, 11, 16, 29, 31, 37, 51, 63, 87
Tydeus, 91
Tyranny, 9
Tyrant, 102

Ulysses, 3, 17, 98; etymology of, 22–23
Understanding, 13, 34, 37, 38, 40–45, 48–53, 57, 59, 69, 73, 76, 81, 86, 99, 106
Underworld, 29–33, 39, 51–57, 79,

82–84, 87, 94, 99, 101–3
Urania, 37, 48

Vehemence, 105
Veins, 9, 36–37
Ventricles, 47
Venus, 6, 7, 10–12, 14, 19, 26, 46–47, 62, 89, 91
Verbal ornament, 4
Verse, 35, 49
Vexation, 13
Vice(s), 4, 7, 12, 13, 22, 28, 32, 38, 39, 44, 46, 48–50, 52, 56–58, 60–101 *passim*, 104–6. *See also individual vices*
Victory, 76–77
Virgil, 3–6, 10, 16, 20, 31, 36, 38, 41, 43, 46, 48, 51, 53, 55, 60–62, 66, 72, 80, 88, 101, 105
Virgin, 43, 57, 68, 71
Virtue(s), 4, 13, 20–24, 28, 29, 32, 38, 40–41, 44, 46, 47, 50, 52, 54, 56, 58, 60–99 *passim*, 101, 105, 106. *See also individual virtues*
Vision, 30, 33, 52, 63, 68
Voice, 37, 54, 64, 67, 87, 94
Volcano, 9–10, 23
Vulcan, 11

Wailing, 13
Walls, 98–101, 104, 106
Wantonness, 96
War, 45, 67, 76, 92, 102
Water, 6, 7, 9, 12, 20, 22, 36, 46, 47, 64–66, 73, 74, 76, 77, 79, 80, 85, 107
Wax, 49

Wealth, 23, 51, 76, 93, 95, 97–98
Weapons, 99, 104–5
Weeping, 13, 15, 57, 64, 90, 100
Wheel, 105
Whirlwind, 9
Wife, 6, 11, 14, 53–55, 89, 98, 104
Wildness, 44
Will, 33, 34, 43, 80, 96
Wind, 7–10, 50, 52, 56, 59, 64, 66, 72, 76, 78–81, 96
Winter, 63, 74, 75, 94
Wisdom, 11, 13, 20, 21, 26, 34, 36–38, 42, 43, 45, 47–51, 53–55, 57, 59, 62–64, 69, 70, 78–80, 83–88, 98, 103, 105, 106
Wise man, 21, 23, 32, 37, 38, 69, 71, 79, 81, 83, 84, 88, 90, 93, 96, 101
Wit, 12, 17, 46–48, 57, 59, 60, 63, 78, 91, 105–7
Women, 10, 13, 14, 46, 88, 89, 93, 97
Word(s), 4, 14, 16, 26, 41, 45, 46, 51, 54, 58, 61, 85, 87, 100
World, 7, 8, 11, 13, 14, 30, 50, 81, 101, 102
World soul, 42
Worship, 41
Writing, 4, 38

Y, letter, 58, 63
Young manhood, 25, 39
Youth, 18, 24, 25, 28, 49

Zetes, etymology of, 71–72
Zodiac, 106